SUPPORTING CHANGE AND DEVELOPMENT

in primary schools

Edited by:
Mike Sullivan

Contributors
Moyra Bentley, R.J. Campbell, Sally
Davies, Eric Dodd, Chris Jones, Ann Lewis,
Brenda Lofthouse, Ruth Merttens, David
Sheppard, David Winkley.

Longman

Published by Longman Industry and Public Service Management,
Longman Group UK Limited, 6th Floor, Westgate House, The High,
Harlow, Essex CM20 1YR, England and Associated Companies
throughout the world.
Telephone: Harlow(0279) 442601
Fax: Harlow(0279)444501
Telex: 81491 Padlog

A catalogue record for this book is available from The British Library

ISBN 0-582-08945-x

Printed and bound in Great Britain by
Biddles Ltd, Guildford and King's Lynn

Contents

Notes on contributors

Moyra Bentley is Senior Lecturer in Education at North Riding College, Scarborough.

R.J. Campbell is Professor of Education at the University of Warwick. His publications include *Developing the Primary School Curriculum*, Holt.

Sally Davies is Headteacher of Priorslee County Primary School, Telford, and formerly Head of Brockton C E School, Shropshire.

Eric Dodd is Deputy Head of a Middle School in Newcastle-Upon-Tyne and was formerly seconded to the Newcastle-Upon-Tyne Appraisal Project.

Chris Jones is Deputy Head of Green Rock Primary School, Walsall, and was formerly seconded to Walsall's ESG Primary Science Team.

Dr Ann Lewis lectures in education at the university of Warwick. Her publications include *Primary Special Needs and the National Curriculum*, Routledge.

Brenda Lofthouse is Head of All Saints CE Primary School, Wellingborough. Joint Editor of the *Study of Primary Education* Series, Falmer.

Ruth Merttens is a Co-Director of IMPACT and lectures at the Polytechnic of North London. She is joint author of *Sharing Maths Cultures*, Falmer.

David Sheppard is County INSET Co-ordinator, Norfolk, and former ILEA Co-ordinator SCDC *Arts in School* Project.

Mike Sullivan is Headteacher of Busill Jones Primary School, Walsall. His publications include *Parents and Schools*, Scholastic.

Dr David Winkley is Headteacher of Grove Junior School, Handsworth, and is Director of the National Primary Centre, Westminster College, Oxford. His publications include *Diplomats and Detectives*, Fulton

Introduction

Mike Sullivan

The demands made upon primary schools and their teachers have grown greatly in the past decade. Direction, advice and guidance comes from all quarters including the Department of Education and Science (DES), the National Curriculum Council (NCC), the Schools Examination and Assessment Council (SEAC), HMI and Local Education Authorities (LEAs). Making sense and putting into context this sometimes confusing and conflicting plethora of information is a daunting task in that it must be undertaken in addition to normal teaching duties.

Teachers are faced with the need to develop a full understanding of their obligations to deliver a broad and balanced curriculum, including the National Curriculum. There is also the need to get to grips with the requirements to assess and test children formally at regular intervals and to develop comprehensive systems of recording progress. The advice is given in general terms, yet each school is a unique mix of staff expertise, community needs and management style. Though the requirements placed on schools are universal, the response that schools make will be very individual as they try to make the best fit between demands and capabilities.

Supporting Change and Development in Primary Schools is aimed at helping schools fashion their own responses to change. Examples are provided of ways in which schools from a variety of different environments have successfully tackled curriculum development. In Chapter 2, Moyra Bentley describes how a number of small schools worked collaboratively to bring together ideas and resources, thereby not only improving their efficiency and effectiveness but also reducing the isolation that teachers in small schools so often experience.

Sally Davies (Chapter 3) describes how, as a new head of a rural school, she developed and implemented forward-looking policies. An area which Sally describes as being particularly important is the 'Curriculum Review' as a means of establishing priorities. The chapter gives practical advice on ways of conducting reviews and the importance not only of involving all the members of staff but of maintaining the support of parents and the community. This is a theme which we return to in 'Developing a partnership with parents' (Chapter 7) and 'New initiatives in primary maths' (Chapter 8).

Changes in the curriculum have created a great increase in pressure on individual teachers and one way of easing the load is for teachers to take on specific responsibility for a particular curriculum area. In Chapter 1, Jim Campbell describes, from case studies, effective ways in which curriculum co-ordinators can support colleagues. In small schools this can still mean that one teacher takes responsibility for a number of substantial curriculum areas; in this situation Moyra Bentley's suggestion of one teacher taking on a specific curriculum responsibility for a number of small schools has a great deal of attraction.

Brenda Lofthouse, in her chapter on 'Curriculum development and change in an urban school' (Chapter 4) explores the politics of the staff room and the need for an understanding of both the 'noble arts' and the 'black arts' in bringing about substantive change. Determination, persistence and even stubbornness are characteristics needed when reason and gentle persuasion fail. Particularly useful is Brenda Lofthouse's Curriculum Development Plan with its emphasis on both review and built-in evaluation. This would certainly form the basis for the construction of a comprehensive 'Whole School Development Plan'. Without sound structure and sets of priorities there is a great danger of becoming overwhelmed by initiatives and of attempting to do too much too quickly.

The traditional role of the LEA Adviser/Inspector in supporting change has altered dramatically. The role is no longer that of a provider of in-service training and support but that of monitoring school and pupil performance through direct observation. Though LEAs still undertake some responsibility for in-service training the provision will inevitably change. Under the arrangements for Local Management of Schools (LMS) there is greater freedom to shop around and purchase training from a variety of sources. Schools are likely to be very selective and will be in the market particularly for support that is shaped to meet their specific needs. The in-service courses delivered at a local Teachers' Centre may soon become events of the past in much the same way as have long-term secondments for award-bearing courses. The temptation may well be to go for a mix and match of courses from a variety of institutions — that is if schools can still afford to send teachers on courses. Alternatively there can be a temptation to try to meet most of the needs by sharing the expertise that already exists on a self-help basis during Baker Days or at other times set aside for staff training. Evaluating the effectiveness of the former and avoiding an over-concentration on pragmatism and parochialism in the latter presents problems.

David Winkley in Chapter 5 strongly believes that much training and support should be provided on a consultancy basis, drawing on expertise not only from educationalists but from those with appropriate skills beyond the conventional boundaries. These consultants would work on a specific task, highlighting both problems and possible solutions from a variety of perspectives. This contributor gives examples on the ways in which he has used consultants in his own inner-city school.

Curriculum development depends greatly on teacher effectiveness and a means of measuring this is through regular teacher appraisal. Eric Dodd was seconded to the Newcastle's teacher appraisal pilot scheme and his contribution (Chapter 6) provides important insights into the positive outcomes that can flow from this process. Particularly valuable are the ways in which the process causes teachers to reflect on their roles and their personal career development. Training needs are identified and the process also enables teachers to identify priorities in resource provision and school management that will enhance their personal contribution to the school. The model that Eric Dodd proposes is a sensitive and valuable tool in strengthening a school and is far more than just a means of 'weeding out poor teachers'.

There is much more to a school than teaching in classrooms and Chapter 7 ('Developing a partnership with parents') looks at ways in which support from parents can be channelled to provide an effective overlap in learning between home and school. Ruth Merttens continues to take up this theme in Chapter 8 and through her work with IMPACT (Inventing Maths for Parents and Children and Teachers) shows ways in which a sustained, enjoyable and effective programme of parental involvement in the teaching of mathematics can be developed. The principles that underlie her work can be applied to extending parental involvement across the curriculum.

Curriculum needs more than breadth, continuity and consistency to be successful, it also needs fully to engage children's interests and imagination. David Sheppard (Chapter 9) explores ways in which drama and art are worth pursuing in their own right and also investigates how they can serve as a means of dynamically developing a whole range of other curriculum areas. The enormous value of conviction, enthusiasm and fun are rarely referred to in official curriculum documents. David Sheppard's work underlines the vitality needed to make teaching and learning a worthwhile experience.

Advisory teachers have an uncertain future and will need to convince schools that what they offer is a good use of funds. Under LMS schools have to establish their own priorities and under the constraints of a tight budget schools may have to balance the cost of the advisory teacher's services against basic stock or a classroom-based teacher. In Chapter 10 Chris Jones draws from his own experience as a support teacher for science on how working shoulder to shoulder with colleagues in classrooms is the very best form of in-service training, not only enhancing the curriculum on a short-term basis, but laying the foundations for sustainable change after the advisory assistance is withdrawn.

The trend is for schools to be self-supporting in more and more areas. The area of curriculum development is no exception. *Supporting Change and Development in Primary Schools* raises issues and provides examples of ways in which schools have met the challenges with which all primary teachers are now confronted. The contributors have drawn from their own extensive and successful experience in describing strategies for maintaining the initiative in curriculum development and giving it a sense of direction.

1 Curriculum co-ordinators and the National Curriculum

R.J. Campbell

Jim Campbell has taken a great interest in the ways that postholders carry out their specialist functions in primary schools. In this chapter he investigates ways in which curriculum co-ordinators can support developments in primary school within the framework of the National Curriculum.

Curriculum co-ordinators: background

The publication of *Primary Education in England*[1] marked the beginning of a decade in which a gradually intensifying interest was focused on the role of teachers with responsibility for an aspect of the curriculum, variously called curriculum postholders, curriculum consultants, subject advisers, and curriculum co-ordinators. I shall standardise on the latter term, since the terminology varies, but not the role specification.

Scattered throughout *Primary Education in England* were references to the importance of the role of curriculum co-ordinators for the quality of pupils' learning, of which the following are significant:

a. Planning programmes of work (4.5–4.6).

b.   Helping teachers match work to children's capacities (7.36).
c.   Developing and maintaining subject expertise to give a lead in curriculum planning (7.37).
d.   Raising the status of the co-ordinators (8.45).
e.   Developing acceptable means of assessing work throughout the school (8.46; 8.58).
f.   The role required time to be allocated for performing the range of duties involved, some of which (keeping up-to-date in a subject for example) assumed time outside school hours, while others needed to be carried out while the school was in sessions (8.47).

The Inspectors summarised their view of the role as follows:

'Teachers in posts of special responsibility need to keep up-to-date in their knowledge of their subject; to be familiar with its main concepts, with the sub-divisions of the subject material, and how they relate to one another. They have to know enough of available teaching materials and teaching approaches to make and advise upon choices that suit local circumstances. And they should be aware of the ways in which children learn and of any sequences of learning that need to be taken into account. Additionally, these teachers should learn how to lead groups of teachers and to help others teach material which is appropriate to the abilities of the children. They should learn how to establish a programme of work in co-operation with other members of staff and how to judge whether it is being operated successfully. They should also learn how to make the best use of the strengths of teachers of all ages and help them to develop so that they may take on more responsibility ....'(8.64)

This expanded and elaborated specification of the co-ordinator's role was presented with the authority of HM Inspectorate. A year after publication of the survey, it appeared to receive the imprimatur of the National Union of Teachers, whose survey about middle schools[2], whatever its ambivalence about the schools themselves, contained illustrative, though not necessarily representative, organisational arrangements from an 8–12 school. It listed the responsibilities of co-ordinators, now called 'subject area consultants', in a way that reflected the recent changes in their role definition (p.10):

a.   to advise on the curriculum and prepare schemes, if necessary, within their particular field of expertise (including books and materials);

b.   to contribute to general curriculum development in the school;
c.   to advise colleagues on any problem of content, background knowledge, sources or method involving their particular field of expertise;
d.   in collaboration with year group leaders to guide probationary teachers; and
e.   whenever appropriate to liaise with colleagues in the first and high schools.

Although this list was perhaps excessively coy about the co-ordinator's role in visiting colleagues' classes to see work in progress, it implicitly seemed to be accepting the wide ranging definition that had already been developed by the Inspectorate. Before that, the *Bullock Report*[3] had stressed the importance it attached to language consultants, and in 1982 the *Cockcroft Report*[4] provided a full job specification for mathematics co-ordinators:

In our view it should be part of the duties of the mathematics co-ordinator to:
prepare a scheme of work for the school in consultation with the headteacher and staff and, where possible, with schools from which the children come and to which they go (we discuss this further in paragraph 363);
provide guidance and support to other members of staff in implementing the scheme of work, both by means of meetings and by working alongside individual teachers;
organise and be responsible for procuring, within the funds made available, the necessary teaching resources for mathematics, maintain an up-to-date inventory and ensure that members of staff are aware of how to use the resources which are available;
monitor work in mathematics throughout the school, including methods of assessment and record-keeping;
assist with the diagnosis of children's learning difficulties and with their remediation;
arrange school-based in-service training for members of staff as appropriate;
maintain liaison with schools from which children come and to which they go, and also with LEA advisory staff.
(from *Mathematics Counts* 1982)

We also had in 1982 the HMI survey on education in first schools[5] in which it was proposed that even for the very youngest children in our school system, curriculum planning and curriculum organisation should be influenced by teachers with special expertise — by curriculum co-ordinators.

Further support for the emerging idea that curriculum co-ordinators should play a central role in developing school-wide curriculum policies came from the committee of enquiry chaired by Thomas into Inner London primary schools.[6] The recommendations of this report included the new proposal that curriculum co-ordination should not necessarily be associated with above-scale payments, but that what the report called the 'dual role' of class teaching and advising colleagues in an aspect of the curriculum should be part of the expectations for virtually all primary school teachers, and that the schools should be staffed in ways that enabled the co-ordinating role to be supported and implemented. A year later, a Select Committee report, *Achievement in Primary Schools*,[7] elaborated on the theme and saw curriculum co-ordination as a key task in the creation of 'whole school development plans'. It also attempted to clarify the terminology arguing for the standardisation of the term 'co-ordinator', and describing the role in practice as follows:

> 9.24   As we have already said, it is too much to expect every teacher to keep up with changes in knowledge and methodology in every field. Each would be helped by having a colleague nearby to turn to for information and help from time to time, and especially so if the roles of adviser and advised could be exchanged on other occasions: i.e. that there was no question of hierarchy.

> 9.25   We envisage that the colleagues giving help should do so in two main ways: by taking the lead in the formulation of a scheme of work; and by helping teachers individually to translate the scheme into classroom practice either through discussion or by helping in the teaching of the children. Much the most frequent method would be discussion. Direct teaching might often take place with the classteacher present, not least so that the classteacher can manage on his or her own next time. But sometimes it might be better to teach the children away from their own teacher because that is easier for the co-ordinator to manage, or because to do so makes it possible to avoid distraction, or because the class teacher could use the time to do something else. If the teaching is done separately, the classteacher should be responsible for ensuring that the work done fits with the rest of the child's programmes. Linkage with the rest of the programme is what matters, not where the teaching takes place. Children near the

end of the primary stage are more likely to need access to additional teachers than are those near the beginning.

9.26 We believe this scenario represents the highest common factor of what various witnesses have put to us and is consistent with what we have seen and been told by teachers in schools. We consider it to be quite unlike the forms of specialist teaching commonly found in secondary schools, though it does allow the possibility of movement between teachers. The most extreme cases we postulate are, on the one hand, a class is taught by the classteacher alone; and on the other, a whole class is taught for a minority of subjects by teachers other than the classteacher, who may or may not be present. In between, and most commonly, a classteacher will be advised by another teacher from time to time; or the co-ordinating teacher will help with the teaching of the class or group of children in the presence of the classteacher; or will take a group of children elsewhere for some aspect of their work.

Curriculum co-ordination: the role in practice

Alongside the official and semi-official sponsorship of an extended role for teacher as curriculum co-ordinators a number of small-scale empirical studies[8] of the role in practice began to be published as well as some self-reports.[9]

My own study[10] attempted to analyse the skills required of curriculum co-ordinators in 10 school-based curriculum initiatives, classified as follows:

Classification of co-ordination skills

I.   *Curricular skills,* that is those skills and qualities involved in knowledge about the curriculum area for which the post-holder has responsibility.

II. *Inter-personal skills,* that is those skills and qualities arising from postholder's relationships with colleagues and other adults.

The sub-divisions are:

I   CURRICULAR SKILLS

   a.   *Knowledge of subject:* the postholder must keep up-to-date in her subject, must know its conceptual structure and methods etc.

b. *Professional skills:* the postholder must draw up a programme of work, manage its implementation, maintain it and assess its effectiveness.

c. *Professional judgement:* the postholder must know about, and discriminate between various materials and approaches in her subject, must relate them to children's development stages, manage the school's resources, and achieve a match between the curriculum and the pupils' abilities.

II. INTER-PERSONAL SKILLS

d. *Social skills:* the postholder must work with colleagues, leading discussion groups, teaching alongside colleagues, help develop their confidence in her subject, advise probationers, etc.

e. *External representation:* the postholder must represent her subject to outsiders, (other teachers, advisers, governors, parents etc.)

(From Campbell, R.J.(1985) *Developing the Primary School Curriculum,* Holt, Rinehart and Winston.)

A more detailed case-by-case analysis (Figure 1) shows the wide range of skills of curriculum co-ordinators that are demanded in practice.

It is worth illustrating by brief versions of case material the nature of the work demands made in particular situations. In Case Study 4, the staff of a multi-ethnic 8–12 middle school followed a school-based programme for a term in which they examined the language of the routine classroom assignments they set for their pupils, using some Open University materials on language as a basis. The overall aim was to increase staff awareness of the difficulties encountered by pupils when they were attempting to carry out normal learning tasks. Ten staff were involved, with at least one from each of the four year groups, and the programme comprised a three-stage sequence as follows:

1. *Staff planning workshop* led by the co-ordinator in which an area of classroom language (e.g. the written language on workcards) was identified as worth focusing upon;

2. *Teachers observed* the language difficulties by selected pupils in carrying out classroom assignments;

3. *Staff evaluation group* led by the co-ordinator in which the observation activities were discussed and analysed, children's problems identified, and possible remedies in terms of teaching techniques suggested.

Figure 1:   Range of skills expected of the curriculum co-ordinators in 10 school-based curriculum developments

SKILLS INVOLVED IN SCHOOL-BASED CURRICULUM DEVELOPMENT	1	2	3	4	5	6	7	8	9	10
I. CURRICULUM SKILLS										
a. *Subject knowledge*										
1. updating subject knowledge	✓	✓		✓		✓	✓	✓		✓
2. identifying conceptual structure of subject(s)	✓		✓			✓	✓	✓		
3. identifying skills in subject(s)	✓		✓	✓		✓	✓	✓	✓	✓
b. *Professional skills*										
4. reviewing existing practice	✓	✓	✓	✓	✓	✓	✓	✓	✓	✓
5. constructing scheme/programme	✓	✓	✓	✓	✓	✓	✓	✓	✓	✓
6. implementing scheme/programme		✓	✓	✓	✓	✓	✓	✓	✓	✓
7. assessing scheme/programme	✓	✓	✓	✓	✓		✓			
c. *Professional judgement*										
8. deciding between available resources	✓	✓	✓	✓	✓	✓	✓	✓	✓	✓
9. deciding about methods	✓	✓	✓	✓	✓	✓	✓	✓	✓	✓
10. identifying links between subjects	✓	✓	✓			✓	✓	✓	✓	
11. ordering, maintaining resources	✓	✓	✓	✓	✓	✓	✓	✓	✓	✓
12. relating subject to its form in other schools	✓		✓	✓		✓			✓	
II. INTER-PERSONAL SKILLS										
d. *Working with colleagues*										
13. leading workshops/discussions	✓	✓	✓	✓	✓	✓	✓	✓		
14. translating material into comprehensible form	✓	✓	✓	✓	✓	✓	✓			
15. liaising with head and/or senior staff	✓	✓	✓	✓	✓	✓	✓	✓	✓	✓
16. advising colleagues informally	✓	✓	✓	✓	✓	✓	✓	✓	✓	✓
17. teaching alongside colleagues	✓				✓	✓	✓	✓		
18. visiting colleagues' classes to see work in progress		✓	✓					✓		
19. maintaining colleagues' morale, reducing anxiety etc.		✓		✓		✓	✓			
20. dealing with professional disagreement	✓	✓	✓	✓		✓				
e. *External representation*										
21. Consulting advisers, university staff etc.	✓	✓		✓	✓	✓				✓
22. Consulting teachers in other schools	✓			✓		✓				✓
23. Consulting parents, governors										

This sequence was repeated three times with three different language topics.

The co-ordinator's role in this development was crucial. She had had to inform herself of some of the recent approaches to language skills (through a post-experience course); she prepared material by rendering it into easily comprehensible form (the 'idiot's pack' as one of the teachers called it), and organised the agenda of meetings in a way that convinced the participants that they would not be wasting their time; she explained and justified the approaches she was encouraging; she maintained morale at a time in the programme when the production of a musical and the school-wide administration of achievement tests had tended to drain the teachers' energies and affect participation, and she helped maintain an attitude and atmosphere in the meetings which was simultaneously business-like and supportive. In fact the staff involved regarded the discussion sessions as probably the most useful of the activities in the programme. As a participant said: 'They were very useful, you had to think about what you were doing with kids and why... it was especially valuable that there was a planning discussion before we did something and then to come back afterwards.'

One of the other teachers commented on the atmosphere in which the meetings were conducted, stressing the sense of solidarity amongst staff: 'I think it's worked well here because we don't mind being shown up — you know we don't mind coming in and saying, "It's been a disaster!" There's no point in doing this kind of thing if you're not going to be honest with one another — pretending you've got perfect results would be a waste of time.'

Above all the teachers valued the expertise and organisational flair of the co-ordinator: 'There would be problems if the discussion sessions had just been started cold. They needed someone who's familiar with the material who knows that background. The last thing I'd want would be where we'd get to the stage where we'd say, "What shall we talk about this week?".'

Case Study 3 provides a particularly clear image of some aspects of the kinds of conflict brought to the surface by school-based development. In this school, a working group of five staff led by the co-ordinator had developed a draft language policy that had implications for the classroom practice of every teacher in the school. For example, the policy required that spelling should be taught more from children's mistakes and less from isolated textbook exercises, and that drama should be incorporated regularly into the curriculum of every class. The working group incorporated staff from different years, had been open to other staff, and had a written record of its meetings open to inspection.

A full staff meeting that concluded the process endorsed the policy as a whole: 'There was a lot of discussion and lots of interest. Because of the detailed content of the working party, and the incorporation of amendments as we went along, there was only one further change agreed at this meeting. But the big thing was that the whole staff agreed that this was to be the policy for the school.'

Nevertheless, in this programme as in six others studied, the co-ordinator experienced conflict and strain in her role, especially in the process of implementing the policy. As part of this process she had been allowed a small amount of time in the week free of teaching to work alongside other teachers, be available to advise them, and to monitor the progress of the policy, through the school. As the co-ordinator saw this aspect of her role, she would be perceived by her colleagues as 'inspecting' the quality of their response to the language policy. The potential for friction arising from this development, even between staff who normally enjoyed warm friendly relationships, was recognised by the co-ordinator, who preferred to withdraw from actively advising and monitoring work in progress, and settle for the staff taking the initiative in seeking advice. The expectations built into the co-ordinator's role here revealed the critically problematic nature of her status in the school, especially in respect of the perceived autonomy of class-teachers.

The empirical studies, despite differences in methodology and problems of representativeness, revealed a number of stresses encountered by co-ordinators attempting to fulfil the new role expectations. These included:

1. *ambiguity in relationships with other classteachers,* whose view of classroom autonomy clashed with the leadership role of the co-ordinator in whole school development;
2. *conflicting priorities,* mainly arising out of inadequate time and facilities for carrying out the co-ordination action role as well as more normal classroom teaching duties;
3. *uncertainty in performing the role of 'educationalist',* that is in articulating the reasons, justifications and 'theory' of a subject in workshop settings, or in representing the rationale of the subject to colleagues, teachers in other schools, and to governors.

Rodger's study[11] illustrated some of the problems encountered by co-ordinators not enjoying full support from the head-teacher; Goodacre[12] argued for the co-ordinators to undertake 'assertiveness training' if they were to fulfil the role adequately;

and based on my research, I concluded that the tasks could be effectively carried out only by untypically talented and committed teachers, given the working conditions in most primary schools.

Discussion: implications for teachers' work

Acknowledgement of the resource needs

What has been experienced in the post-1978 period is a kind of galloping inflation in the co-ordinator's role. This inflation has been in five areas:

a. an increase in the significance attached to the role of the curriculum co-ordinator for raising quality and standards in the curriculum;
b. increased importance of subject specialisation and subject expertise;
c. increased complexity of the job of curriculum co-ordination in practice;
d. increased potential for conflict and strain in the role in practice;
e. increased importance of what I have called above 'Interpersonal Skills', in implementing change.

Since the early 1980s, the government, HMI and others have begun to face the policy and resource implications of the new role, and to acknowledge some of the problems flowing from current working conditions. Two HMI surveys, on 9–13 middle schools and on 8–12 middle schools,[13] explicitly acknowledged the problem of teacher time as a major obstacle. The report on ILEA primary schools, *Improving Primary Schools*,[14] which recommended the dual role for virtually all teachers, irrespective of position on the salary scales, also recognised the need to improve staffing, probably by about 10%, if the role was to become feasible. In principle moreover, the Government 1985 White Paper *Better Schools*[15] accepted that primary school teachers 'had the strongest claim for additional time' free from teaching. Perhaps most important of all, the House of Commons Select Committee,[16] at the end of 1986, noted that at least 15 000 extra teachers were needed for co-ordination tasks, amongst other things, and reported that Sir Keith Joseph, when Secretary of State for Education, had confirmed this figure. Coming at what then seemed like the end of a long period of industrial unrest in the education service, recognition of the importance of resourcing co-ordination tasks appeared to promise a real chance of realising the potential in the role, and of developing 'collegiality' in primary schools. Such promise was broken by Kenneth Baker's abrupt dismissal of the Select Committee proposals for resourcing, given in a Parliamentary Memorandum in December 1987.

Teachers' working conditions

There is also the impact of the Teachers' Pay and Conditions Act 1987. From the point of view of curriculum co-ordination, the new conditions of service seemed supportive, for they made some in-school development possible by incorporating it into the normal duties and responsibilities of teachers. The five 'Baker Days' per year, although presently perhaps conceived of in a rather mechanistic way, nonetheless provide a significant improvement in teachers' working conditions since they identify time free of teaching contractually assured, that could be used for the development of whole school curriculum policies. Shortage of time, as the empirical studies revealed, was a major perceived obstacle to such development.

This is a start, but only a start. Other aspects of the working conditions of teachers still require attention, including especially the fabric of the buildings, and the reprographic and other facilities available to them. And there are still two major problems: of curriculum expertise in the teaching force, especially expertise in science and technology; and of morale in the profession, as yet not recovered from the impact of industrial action and the destruction of its negotiating rights over pay and conditions.

The National Curriculum and curriculum co-ordinators

It might be thought that the imposition of a National Curriculum had set all the development activities in schools at nought; that attainment targets, programmes of study and assessment arrangements, specified in considerable detail would render the role of curriculum co-ordinators redundant. Even at an early stage in the establishment of the National Curriculum, this would be a dangerous mis-reading of the political context of primary school teachers' work in the early 1990s. On the contrary, the establishment of the National Curriculum makes the role of curriculum co-ordinators even more significant.

This is because, firstly, the National Curriculum, defined in subject terms, is specified as a *planning* model, not an *implementation* model. There is no intention to specify how the curriculum will be 'delivered' in any particular school and no requirement in law that given proportions of time should be allocated to particular subjects. The organisation and implementation of the curriculum remains a key task for a school's staff. Moreover, it is impossible, or at least unwise, for curriculum planning to be other than whole school planning for consistency and continuity. The quality of curriculum leadership by co-ordinators is at a premium in such planning.

Secondly, the skill that has been called 'External Representation' in Figure 1, i.e., 'representing the subject to outsiders', becomes increasingly important. This is because the pressure to account to parents, governors and others for aspects of the curriculum in a school takes on heightened significance as it becomes a legal requirement. Curriculum co-ordinators now find themselves important contributors to annual meetings, and to governing bodies' meetings, as well as to less formal activities such as workshops for parents and colleagues in the relevant curriculum area.

In a consumerist climate of open enrolment and effective parental choice, the ability of co-ordinators to deliver accounts to the school's consumers (or at least to be successful public relations' practitioners on the school's behalf), has become a crucial factor in securing or maintaining the confidence of a school's community.

Thirdly there is a substantial role for co-ordinators in helping a school's staff develop systematic approaches to classroom assessment.[18] Although much of the criticism of the proposed National Curriculum has concentrated on the aspect of national 'testing' at ages seven and 11, the Bill itself is concerned with 'assessment arrangements'. These will include standardised assessment tasks from a national bank, but most assessment for most of the primary school pupils' life will be subjective classroom-based assessment. Within an overall and convincingly delivered strategy for pupil assessment, the problems associated with 'testing', and particularly with the public reporting of assessment results, can be mitigated. Once again this calls for effective and informed leadership by curriculum co-ordinators, if primary schools are to be delivered from the fragmentary, casual and often negligent manner in which pupils' progress was previously assessed in the school curriculum.

None of this is easy, but, as is often the case, pioneering schools with talented co-ordinators have led the way. They have revealed some of the potential, and many of the pitfalls of curriculum co-ordination. The National Curriculum will impose greater direction, and bring greater pressure, on primary schools to build upon what has been learned since 1978, rather than to abandon the achievements, admittedly patchily and haltingly created, of individual schools and co-ordinators. As Richards[19] has commented, the intention of policies for co-ordinators in primary schools is to 'support not undermine' class teaching. Such support is going to be increasingly needed as schools implement the National Curriculum.

References

1   DES (1978) *Primary Education in England*, HMSO, London.
2   NUT (1979) *Middle Schools: Deemed or Doomed?*, London.
3   Committee of Enquiry into Reading and the Used of English, *A Language for Life* (Bullock Report) (1984), HMSO, London.
4   Committee of Enquiry into the Teaching of Mathematics in Schools, *Mathematics Counts*, (Cockcroft Report)(1982), HMSO, London.
5   DES (1982) *Education 5–9*, HMSO, London.
6   ILEA (1985) *Improving Primary Schools*, London.
7   House of Commons (1986) *3rd Report of the Education, Science and Arts Committee, Achievement in Primary Schools*, HMSO, London.
8   e.g. Campbell R.J. (1983) *Developing the Primary School Curriculum* (Holt, Rinehart and Winston, London, 1985), Primary Schools Research and Development Group, *Curriculum Responsibility and the Use of Teacher Expertise in the Primary School*, University of Birmingham. Rodger, I. et al.(1983) *Teachers With Posts of Responsibility in Primary Schools*, University of Durham.
9   e.g. Dodds, D. and Armstrong, G. 'Developing a Junior School Science Programme' *Education 3–13*, 13(1), pp. 17–21; and Heritage, M. (1985) 'Curriculum Change: a school-based approach' *Education 3–13*, 13(1), pp. 22–25.
10 Campbell, R.J. (1985) *Developing the Primary School Curriculum*, Holt, Rinehart and Winston, London.
11 Rodger, I. et al. (1983) *Teachers with Posts of Responsibility in Primary Schools*, University of Durham.
12 Goodacre, E. (1984) 'Language Postholders and assertiveness' *Education 3–13*, 12(1), pp. 17–21.
13 DES (1983) *9–13 Middle Schools*, HMSO, London; and DES (1985) *Education 8–12 in combined and Middle Schools*, HMSO, London.
14 ILEA (1985) *Improving Primary Schools*, London.
15 White Paper (1985) *Better Schools* HMSO, London.
16 House of Commons, (1986) *3rd Report of the Education Science and Arts Committee*, HMSO, London.
17 DES (1987) *The National Curriculum 5–16: A Consultative Document*, HMSO, London.
18 Burgess, H. (1987) 'Springing free from formal assessment, *Education 3–13*, 13(1).
19 Richards, C. (1986) 'The curriculum from 5–16: implications for primary school teachers' *Education 3–13*, 15(1).

2 Amplifying the educational opportunities in small rural schools

Moyra Bentley

Moyra Bentley describes a project that linked together a group of 15 small rural schools and seven town schools. As the project's independent evaluator, the author provides objective insights into the mechanisms of collaboration. The project's funding enabled the schools to employ jointly two teachers, a non-teaching assistant and also to purchase expensive resources for shared use.
The imaginative use of staff and resources may well serve as a model for similar developments under LMS.

Working in a small rural primary school is both very rewarding and immensely challenging. The challenge lies in addressing the disadvantages which this type of school faces. Some of the main problems associated with such schools may be listed as follows:

a. coping with vertically grouped classes;
b. shortage of curriculum expertise;
c. shortage of expensive resources;
d. inadequate buildings;
e. a headteacher who has a heavy teaching commitment;
f. very small peer groups;
g. professional isolation of staff;
h. difficult or long journeys to the nearest in-service centre.

Over recent years there have been a number of local initiatives which have lent support to small rural schools[1]. In 1985, central government also recognised that these schools required specific systems of support and development. Funds became available through the education support grant system to finance local authority projects which aimed to '... improve the quality and range of curriculum provided in primary schools in rural areas'.

North Yorkshire with its large number of two- and three-teacher schools, many of them in remote geographical areas, put in two successful bids, one of which was the Eskdale Project. This bid was not predicated on a position of static curriculum development in the area. Already existing were some self-initiated developments affecting a group of small schools or a small school linked to a larger school in the nearest small town. These took the form of joint sporting arrangements, residential trips, supporting one another in school plays or participating together in theatre, art or musical occasions. Such links will be familiar to many people working in small rural schools throughout the country. In Eskdale, the primary adviser was particularly sympathetic to and supportive of these schools and he had also played an important role in encouraging schools to develop collaboratively as far as possible, though without extra resourcing. This adviser was responsible for developing the bid in conjunction with a small number of headteachers from the area.

In January 1986 the Area Education Officer informed the 15 rural schools that the bid had been successful. In addition five larger town schools and two local secondary schools (11–14 years) were included in the schools listed within the bid. They were thought to be important for their possible resource support and for the liaison advantages their involvement could bring. Their inclusion in the original bid was farsighted as they have proved to be of considerable importance to the successful development of the Project, as will be seen later. The funding was for a quarter of a million pounds over five years, beginning from September 1986. Seventy per cent of this was government money, the remainder was provided by the LEA. This money has to pay for staffing, the lease of a minibus over the whole period, coach transport, supply cover, resources, and the setting up of a base. The staffing totals three — a Project Leader with curriculum strengths in mathematics, design technology, environmental studies and science; another advisory teacher with curriculum strengths in a range of arts areas; and a non-teaching assistant to give clerical support and drive the minibus.

The purposes of the support unit had been theorised in the bid as:

providing additional curriculum expertise;
working closely with headteachers and teachers to develop existing
good practice;
extending the curriculum skills of staff;
encouraging and promoting teacher exchanges;
helping pupils to develop academically, physically and socially;
helping schools to make the best of all the resources available.

Accountability in relation to these purposes was also built into the bid. Financial monitoring was to be done at the local Area Education Officer level. An internal evaluation was to be provided by the participants in conjunction with the Advisory Service, and an independent evaluation to be undertaken by myself on behalf of North Riding College.

All the staff were in post for September 1986. Their first task was to establish a base in a disused schoolhouse attached to one of the Project schools. Teaching rooms, office space and storage were made available. And so the growth and development extant in the area received its fertiliser of enrichment. The Project was ready to roll.

How does the Project operate?

Initially, as with other such projects,[1] there was a certain amount of anxiety and suspicion amongst some headteachers and teachers. A major concern was that both their professional autonomy and school individuality were under threat. However, through sensitive planning and discussion meetings with heads, and through tactful visits to all individual schools, the Project was soon operating at a whirlwind level of activity with a momentum which has not abated. Ownership of the direction of the Project was very clearly in the hands of the participants. It is to the credit of the LEA that from the Project's inception it adopted a stance of trusting in the professional judgement of the teachers and allowing them to be proactive in determining their own lines of development and improvement, as Sigsworth & Bell (1987) advocate:

'There is a ... crucial need for local authorities to appraise the posture they are prepared to adopt in relation to the school-focused nature of small school co-operation ... to repose trust in the professional integrity and judgement of teachers and to provide them with a framework for action which, whilst it grants them freedom of action, also contains an element of accountability.'[1]

The Eskdale Project is one of a number throughout the country which could be described as a 'larger co-operative group'. It has permanent co-ordinating staff and, within the large co-operative group, smaller collaborative groups or clusters of schools form to share such things as expertise, resources, joint project work, peer grouping, INSET, or policy development.

'This pattern of a large co-operative group of schools, well-resourced by the county and with permanent support staff, which allows for the co-operation within it of smaller groups of neighbouring schools, appears to have much to commend it. Certainly it is working well in a number of authorities ...'[2]

The advisory teachers

A large part of the advisory teacher's work involves teaching a series of half-day sessions, anything from two to seven or eight sessions to classes of infants or juniors as requested. The work will be carefully planned jointly with the resident class teacher; some form of team teaching usually takes place. The work is also carefully evaluated as it progresses.

It is often the case that the planning and evaluation of such collaborative work is problematic in view of the lack of time to pay attention to anything other than doing the teaching. However, although there are instances of planning and evaluation being the casualties of the teaching process in the Eskdale Project, nevertheless it is the case they are given high priority and time is spent either in the school or at the Project base planning and evaluating. Although such collaborative talk often takes place before school, during lunchtime and after school, teachers can meet with the advisory teachers at the Project base with the benefit of supply cover if necessary, which is invaluable. This collaborative approach is a major way in which the children's curriculum is being developed and teacher expertise is being strengthened. One example of a typical day for each of the advisory teachers will serve to illustrate this approach (see table).

Although they teach much of the time, they undertake many other roles too. They support curriculum development policy decisions, join residential visits, help plan and take part in project work out of doors, deliver resources, provide a 'sounding-board for ideas', organise the larger group meetings of headteachers and separate meetings of infant teachers and do in-service work. Even this exhausting list is not complete, but gives some idea of how they operate to support and enrich the curriculum of children in small schools.

Thursday, Jan. 21st

Morning

RW is at Grosmont school doing some maths problem-solving work with the junior children. This is one of three sessions. As a result of the input the class teacher feels able to extend and develop the work further on his own.

Afternoon

RW travels to work with the infant teacher of a three-teacher school on science. This is part of a much longer series of sessions. The teacher lacked confidence with science work, but is acquiring confidence and knowledge as a result of these sessions. She is building up a dossier of information, including examples of children's work so that she can recall what to do. She mentions that she is learning a lot about 'asking open-ended questions' and is formulating an infant science curriculum policy document with RW's help alongside the teaching sessions.

MF is at Sleights School working with upper juniors on a large tapestry/collage which will be on display alongside one from each of the Project schools later in the year when the Festival Whitby Abbey 1989 is celebrated. She is using materials and techniques new to the teacher who will be able to use the knowledge more generally in her art and craft work in the future. There are six of these sessions.

MF travels to Lealholm School to do art and craft work with infants in connection with their topic on Scotland. There are four sessions for this.

The town schools and the secondary schools

Again, only a few examples can be given which may further illustrate the variety of ways in which development and change occurs. Throughout the course of the year, the fourth year children of every Project school visit their transfer secondary school for CDT technology sessions taught by the secondary school staff, who can get supply cover through the Project. Not only is this valuable in subject terms, but the obvious transfer benefits are noteworthy too. These schools have also made members of staff available to visit or work in the primary schools which is also known to be 'good transfer practice'.

A number of the town primary schools regularly all year make their halls available to small schools for PE. The minibus is used to transport the children. Another way in which help was offered was when an infant teacher from a two-teacher school wanted some experience of nursery to enable her to cope more adequately with the four-year-olds in her small, vertically-grouped infant classroom. She was invited to spend a half day each week, with her own four-year-olds, in a town nursery for a time. The Project is able to provide supply cover for her. She feels that she has a much better understanding of the needs of children of nursery age and has adapted her classroom and her organisation to take account of what she has learned. Her room is too small for her to be able to 'work miracles' but, nevertheless, the experience was profitable for her and for the children she took with her.

Groupings

Three types of group will be discussed. First, there is the headteachers' group which began by meeting twice termly, but now only feels the need to meet once termly. Sometimes a representative of the secondary schools is present at these meetings which take place in an afternoon at Whitby Teachers' Centre. This is the forum for exchanging views and evaluating the direction and performance of the Project. Many interesting items for discussion appear on the formal agenda, such as plans for in-service for the large collaborative group or information on new resources bought by the Project. Of course, much valuable educational discussion occurs at an informal level at meetings such as these, and these can be the start of many joint initiatives at the smaller cluster group level at which the Project operates, such as sharing a potter-in-residence, for example.

The second grouping is that of smaller clusters of schools. The example that pertains to all of them is that they have made joint purchases of such items as overhead projectors, Casio keyboards, concept keyboards, binocular microscopes, videos and fiction books, which are owned by the Project and shared among the cluster. Working together is another way in which the clusters function. One group of infant teachers from four schools have pursued a joint summer project over the last three years. This involves four full-day outdoor visits, with each infant teacher taking responsibility for organising one of them. The Project pays for the transport and the Project staff accompany the visits and may sometimes help with follow-up work in schools too. A different example is provided by one cluster which used supply cover for one day for the heads so that they could get together to discuss their responses to the National Curriculum science and mathematics documents. A final example is provided by two neighbouring small schools joining with a town school to engage in a week's exchange visit with children from Birmingham. This was also supported by the Project in terms of transport, supply and expertise as the Project Leader went to Birmingham for the week and was involved in the preliminary work in the host schools. He was also involved during the week of the return visit of the Birmingham children which involved a lot of environmental work in the area.

The third grouping is that of the infant teachers and they operate within two groups, one which meets during one afternoon a term and requires supply cover, and another, composed largely of the same people, which meets after school once or twice per term. It only involves infant teachers as every head of a small school in the area teaches the junior age range, an arrangement which is commonplace in many village schools. The afternoon meeting always begins with visits in small groups to another school. Everyone then comes together in one school on a rotational basis to have some in-service, or look at CDT equipment, or to choose more large play equipment to add to that already purchased by the Project and rotating around their schools. The afternoon meeting has more of an in-service approach and indeed, although generated and organised initially by the Project, it is now incorporated into the normal in-service funding of the LEA which is an indication of its perceived value.

Resources, including transport

The minibus is in constant use. It is used regularly to transport children for their CDT work as already mentioned, and five of the small schools with no PE facilities are also taken regularly to schools which have such facilities. There is also the 'visits' use where a school can book the minibus for a whole- or half-day visit to enrich ongoing school work .It is used after school for sporting and other events, and even has occasional weekend or holiday use by the Project schools. In relation to other resources, as well as the cluster purchases already mentioned, the Project has been building up a very fine resource bank at its schoolhouse base. The democratic philosophy which permeates the Project has meant that these purchases have not been made unilaterally. A 'Resources & Publicity Group' was set up at the beginning of the Project. It has representation from each of the clusters, and from heads and teachers. The period of service is four terms and each retiring member finds his or her own replacement. It is this group which recommends to the Project staff what items should be bought. The Project has collected an excellent range of resources such as cagoules and overtrousers, musical instruments, computer software, CDT tools, a video camera, stage blocks and lighting and many other items which small schools could not afford in most instances. The fact that this equipment is fully utilised demonstrates the wisdom of the choices made. A similar approach was adopted when large infant play equipment such as a Brio train set, Duplo house and a Lego road were bought, this time with all the infant teachers involved in the decision-making.

What do the participants think about the project?

Perhaps the first remark to make is that everyone involved is immensely positive and has virtually no criticism to make of the way the Project has developed. To those of us who have been long involved in education generally, and in curriculum development work in particular, this state of affairs seems a rather incredible one, and yet it is the case. Even when directly asked to think of 'concerns' or 'constructive criticism', nothing emerges. One teacher summarised the views of everyone when she said: 'RW runs the scheme as perfectly as anyone can. It works largely because he is so organised and so committed. I cannot think of any aspect of it I would want to change.'

In order to have a framework to discuss the perceptions people have of the effectiveness of the Project, it will be helpful to consider again those supposed needs of small schools.

Breakdown of isolation and making links

There is no doubt that the success of the Project in achieving its purposes is due to the combination of personal qualities and pro-fessional traits exhibited by the Project team, together with the particular self-initiated stage of development that teachers had achieved in the area for themselves which meant that on the whole they were open and receptive to change. As Addison (1982) says about similar developments in Northamptonshire:

'...there is no doubt that the main reason for the changing attitudes is the way in which the advisory teachers in different ways established confident relationships and showed by example what could be achieved with children given some of the resources now at their disposal.'[3]

This ephemeral yet omnipresent feature 'relationships' in primary education discourse is not exceptional. But it is important to note how centrally it characterises why people feel that the Project has been as successful as it has been in final curriculum terms for children. For no matter whether resources, transport, expertise or the breaking-down of isolation is concerned, 'relationships' figure prominently in explaining why the whole thing 'works'. Relationships could not have developed as well as they have done were it not for the tact and sensitivity displayed by the advisory teachers. Campbell (1985) talks of the importance of personal qualities in anyone who is in the role of giving other teachers support as this is such a sensitive political area in a system which has traditionally upheld the autonomy of the class teacher. His remarks pertain equally to advisory teachers working from outside schools as to postholders working from within:

'...(These skills) in addition to demanding considerable charm and character, also required sensitivity and tact, and a number of headteachers made the point that such *personal qualities* in the postholders were prerequisites for the successful implementation of the development.'[4]

That their sensitivity has been noted and appreciated by the teachers is abundantly clear, as is their appreciation of their reliability, enthusiasm, resourcefulness, expertise and their sheer 'hard graft'. Their integrity in not discussing one school with another is a further identified important quality that means that heads and teachers can unburden themselves to them 'safely'. So, whether they are just dropping off a piece of equipment or teaching a half-term's programme of work, or just acting as a 'sounding-board for ideas', the advisory teachers break down isolation and provide the psychological comfort, again strongly featured, of 'just knowing that someone's there'. As another teacher phrased it, 'it takes away the feeling of working in a vacuum'.

Of course, the breaking-down of isolation is not confined to relationships between schools and advisory teachers: 'The most important thing has been the liaison with other teachers ... so welcome is the realisation that others are in similar positions.'

This *'pulling together more'*, as one teacher phrased it, seems particularly welcomed by the infant teachers. Previously, heads met at a termly meeting and at other events, but the opportunity for infant teachers to visit other schools and relate to other infant teachers was a novelty at first. Referring to other infant teachers in her cluster, one teacher said:'We're long past the stage of not admitting fallibility.'

This, of course, is a very healthy educational state to be in.

There are other areas in which relationships are developing to the ultimate benefit of the pupils. The links with secondary schools have already been mentioned, and links with school communities have been strengthened through the efforts made to help parents, governors and the public at large to understand what the purpose of the Project is and to convince people of its value. Certainly the Project would be less successful if parents were unhappy about another teacher being involved in teaching their child, other children of the same age from another school joining their child for some particular peer-group work, or seeing their children on a minibus once a week for swimming or PE. Fortunately consciousness within the community of the value of such events has been raised. That is not to say that every parent has been convinced yet, but then, whenever is that the case?

Although it may seem odd to mention within-school relation-ships under the heading of 'breaking down isolation', it is never-theless pertinent to do so. For a number of school staffs have mentioned how the advent of the Project has made for increased talking and sharing within the school than previously.'We seem to talk to each other more and are more willing to share' is identified as a spin-off. One teacher (not a head) said: 'We are much more open and willing to help one another. We thought about our own expertise and what we could offer one another, rather than getting it in from outside...we even send round our half-term plans to one another and ask for people's comments.'

Finally, it is important to mention the coming-together of pupils. Although talk of teachers coming together or resources being used implicitly means the enhancement of the curriculum of the children, pupils being brought together is a direct influence on them in this area of breaking down isolation and insularity. The four infant teachers who do their summer project together take great delight in the mixing of the children, in the idea that the children are comfortable with any one of them, and that they can choose to put them in a larger peer group if they want to. As one of them said: 'Although there are many benefits of a vertically-grouped class, it is good to be able to have single-peer groups sometimes. When we were doing this raft thing, all the five-year-olds were together and they didn't have any older ones to rely on. They really had to think and to work things out for themselves. It was a delight. It occasionally does them good just to be with their peer group.'

Augmentation of resources

The additional resources, especially transport, loomed large in teachers' articulation of what they found most valuable about the Project. Transport was either valued because it enabled a regular event such as PE or CDT at other schools to take place, or because it was seen as a means of 'enriching' children's education because of the first-hand experiences such travelling could bring about. More recently, the new schools charging policy has been brought in, and quite a significant number of headteachers commented that educational visits would be severely restricted and education impoverished were it not for the minibus, and for the fact that each school is allowed one coach per term for such visits under the Project.

The resources which are provided at three levels are also vastly appreciated and, more to the point, used. An answerphone machine makes school borrowing at the first level, that is the resources based at the Project base, easy to implement. The second level is the cluster purchases which, selected as they are by their users, means that items are constantly in use. And finally, the advisory teachers equip themselves for any work undertaken in schools and so, as one head said: 'They are resourcing all the time, bringing things in that small schools could not afford.'

Another head said that she saw the Project as 'one big resource centre' but she included human resources in this definition and, by doing so, she spoke for many others who wanted to include human resources and expertise under the heading of 'resources'.

Development and enhancement of teacher expertise

Three important points emerge from a consideration of what teachers have to say about the fulfilment of this particular need. One is that they do not define expertise purely in subject terms. Secondly, they find describing the process by which expertise develops difficult, and thirdly, they are certain nevertheless that expertise has developed over the last few years.

In a study of the Project undertaken by the Project Leader he found that:

'The development of teacher expertise then was not seen by the respondents as purely the development of specialist curriculum areas but development of the teacher in the widest sense — reflecting their own practice against that of another teacher working with her children.'[5]

Indeed, one of the teachers he spoke to had this to say:

'Even though expertise may not be increased in a definable way, questioning and observing your children's work with another teacher, or in a different way, inevitably leads to increased expertise. This is not definable in subject terms.'[5]

This, of course, is not to deny that there is such a thing as subject expertise, for clearly there is, but it is important to note their wider definition of expertise, especially in such a time of subject-dominated curriculum talk.

In terms of description of the process by which the development of expertise comes about, 'osmosis', a word used by the Project Leader, seems apt. This covers a multiplicity of ways in which teachers learn to absorb new techniques, new approaches or new knowledge. It can be just as a result of a conversation with another teacher, or noticing the work done by another teacher and asking, 'How did you do that?' through to more formal ways. These include INSET that the advisory teachers organise or run and joint planning, teaching and evaluation of work in and out of classrooms. There is rightly strong resistance to any notions that development of expertise could be measured or quantified in some way. Professional judgement is at work and teachers 'know' that they have developed in a variety of ways and through a variety of means.

Having acknowledged the breadth of the teachers' definitions of expertise, whose development would encompass such examples as the one given earlier of the infant teacher learning how to pose questions differently, some instances relating to subject areas will be examined. Educationalists who are concerned that the curriculum may continue to show signs of undervaluing the arts would be comforted to know that there is no such imbalance revealed by this Project's usage. Both advisory teachers are in full and equal demand and, moreover, Project money which is used to pay for outside expertise is invariably spent on supporting the arts in schools by resourcing such as a potter, a composer, authors and actors to work with the children.

Teachers desirous of developing or enhancing their expertise in science and design technology, using the Project Leader, pre-dates the advent of the National Curriculum, and this possibly accounts for such remarks as: 'Oh yes, I'm much more confident in dealing with national curriculum science, and CDT when it comes, because of the help I've had from RW, and because in the future I know he's there.'

In trying to explain why they feel more confident and more knowledgeable many teachers make comparisons between the effectiveness of INSET and having the support of a good advisory teacher. The results were unfavourable to INSET, even with the newer school-focused approaches: 'I would rather have the Project than GRIST' and 'What the Project offers is so much better than INSET — there's no comparison' and 'It's INSET at its best because it's at the chalk-face — it's using their expertise with your children in your setting with your organisation'.

What I have termed the 'localness factor' is very important to the successful imparting of expertise. As the Project Leader said, he is often meeting the challenge of 'I bet you can't do that in my school/classroom!' and rising to that challenge brings worthwhile and lasting developments in expertise. Even when an out-of-school INSET course runs, such as one done by the Project leader on CDT for Project infant teachers, the participants value it more highly than previous INSET because: 'RW knows us and he knows our situation and our children. It's so much better' and 'The course was actually geared for infant teachers. So often courses say that they're for infant teachers and you get there and it's always geared towards the junior children, whatever they've said. This was different and it was really good'.

I wonder how many infant teachers would find a resonance with that complaint about the age phasing of INSET?

Another important factor is the 'concentratedness' of the advisory teachers. Often such teachers are thinly spread, a particular problem in large rural authorities like North Yorkshire. The Project leader summed up the views of many in this way: 'There are not many agencies to which teachers can refer and know that they are *assured* of a quick response which will be of practical help.'

And, of course, although it is the teachers who receive the support, it is the pupils who are ultimately benefiting from that growth and development which transforms the teacher permanently.

Some general issues for consideration

Although the focus of this chapter has been supporting small schools, there are some general points to be raised which may apply more widely to the process of supporting curriculum change in primary schools. The first issue is one of overwhelming importance although, as yet, perhaps for obvious reasons, not of significance as far as literature about curriculum change is concerned. I am referring to the significance of teachers' personal qualities to the process of 'making things happen'. As one headteacher stated rather baldly: 'The (personal) chemistry element is very important to the notion of any form of collaboration — money won't necessarily encourage it and lack of money won't necessarily prevent it.'

Although this does not address how much more effective and profitable collaboration can be when both good 'chemistry' and extra resources come together, nevertheless the point is a valuable one. So much curriculum change discourse occurs as if teachers were not actually people with human foibles, failings, fears and strengths, and possibly a cultural reticence about promulgating the latter! We need to take much more account of this notion that 'primary teachers are primarily people'[6] in order to come to a deeper understanding of the processes of change.

The second point concerns the notion of 'collaboration' which was used by the headteacher in the last quote. This word is in danger of becoming a shibboleth of primary education discourse, as Alexander (1989)[7] aptly describes it. If a school is not clustering, or collaborating, at present then the educational 'frown of disapproval' is directed its way! The point is not that collaboration is unnecessary or a 'bad thing', but simply that it should have a purpose and, where professionals are judged to be trusted to make appropriate decisions, should they choose not to collaborate for their own good reasons, this decision should be respected. Teachers reported on the 'exhortation to collaborate' for INSET or for curriculum policy-making in particular, but wanted to make the point that this was not always helpful and can even inhibit progress. This point was made by one head who has collaborated closely with a neighbouring school which has a very similar philosophy over a number of things such as shared project work, and joint residential and sporting events: 'No, I couldn't cope with collaboration in curriculum policy development work — it just isn't productive enough and time is so precious... It can sometimes be helpful but can also have very little depth.'

Other headteachers expressed similar views. It is as if all schools, including small schools, have their own 'shopping list of needs' as one head put it. Where these coincide then, for example, school-focused INSET may be the answer. But there are other times when teachers want to be 'school-based' and feel that it is legitimate to pursue development internally.

An interesting mix of 'chemistry' and 'collaboration' can, of course, lead to teachers wishing they were in a different cluster. Geography tends to dictate cluster groupings, but then it can lead to such statements as: 'The infant teachers do more together in this cluster than the junior teachers. It isn't that we don't get on, but somehow I don't feel I relate as well to them as I do to Mrs X or Mr Y who are in a different cluster' or 'I'm not sure that I would find meeting more as an infant cluster or trying to work more closely with Mrs T as worthwhile as I would like. She gives me the impression of superconfidence and that she is getting on so well with her own practice and it makes me feel a bit inadequate. I don't feel that there's the proper atmosphere of trust and humility in which to really talk about problems openly and honestly'.

However well founded in fact or otherwise, those feelings of discomfort for that teacher are genuine and, as long as they remain, the culture of collegiality in that cluster will not develop to the extent of the infant cluster mentioned earlier. It is difficult to see who or what the catalyst might be to bring about the subtle change in relationship which is necessary for those two neighbouring schools to be more supportive of one another. Similar problems exist of course within a larger school.

Another point for general consideration is the reluctance, as evidenced by its virtual lack of occurrence, of teachers leaving their classes to be elsewhere, whether to give or to receive 'expertise'. Although one example was given earlier of an infant teacher visiting a nursery, albeit with a few of her children, such examples are difficult to find, despite an initial aim in the bid to promote teacher exchanges, and despite the fact that supply cover can be made available under the Project. There may be a number of reasons for this. Although the definition of a primary teacher's work role has altered considerably in a short period of time to be much more 'subject reliant', many class teachers are reluctant to take on the mantle of expert to the extent of 'showing other teachers how it's done'. Not only is it possible that such a reticence is culturally endemic, but also there is the fear of 'failing publicly' in another teacher's situation. Certainly such hostility is not unknown in the primary world. Although such hostility is not a threat to most of the teachers in the Project schools, nevertheless there is a characteristic unwillingness to admit to strengths capable of being shared with other teachers or given to other children.

A further inhibitor of such a development is the reluctance many teachers, especially infant teachers, have about not being with their classes.It can operate at the level of 'Anyone but me with my children is a total disaster', which probably has more to do with Alexander's (1984) characterisation of class teaching as 'post hoc rationalisation' rather than any real problems which ensue from a half-day's absence.[8] In this connection, it is interesting to speculate whether small rural school teachers are more reluctant to leave their classes than their urban counterparts where children have relationships with a greater number of adults. Another more justifiable reason is the amount of time new demands are making on INSET in school time. Teachers are here rightly worried about causing even more disruption to their classes than necessary. There will be other legitimate reasons why teachers do not feel happy about the idea of leaving their classes. As Campbell (1985) says in relation to the similar position of postholders, for them it 'raised questions of priority as well as feasibility'.[4] Nevertheless he continues to recommend it as one of a number of options available to teachers to deal with the new subject requirements of the National Curriculum[9] and certainly it would be helpful to learn more of successful examples of teacher exchange or teachers supporting other teachers in their classrooms, including analysis of why it works in those circumstances, in order that such ideas can be disseminated amongst teachers in schools of all sizes.

Conclusion

As mentioned in the introduction to this chapter, the Project's central concern is with curriculum development and enhancement at a time when curriculum seems very much concerned with the development of children's intellect in a number of subject areas or disciplines. There are a number of complex reasons why this happens to be the case at present, some of them more legitimate than others. The point to be made here though is that curriculum is interpreted much more widely than this by these teachers and I would want to support this richer interpretation, just as I would want to support a definition of 'expertise' which also goes beyond the subject matter. This is not an anti-subject stand, although I would like to see more evidence of a substantial debate than appears to have preceded the National Curriculum about the epistemological, sociological and psychological considerations which affect what kinds of knowledge should count in the primary curriculum. It certainly seems that the Project teachers equate curriculum with children's planned, and sometimes unplanned, experiences of being a pupil, and they are as concerned with their emotional, social, moral, spiritual and physical development as they are with their intellectual development. All these teachers seemed to be concerned with questions about what these children are like as people and what kind of people, and what kind of a world, they would like the children to grow up into. Although the idea of 'holistic education' needs much more critical thought applied to it, as part of that move away from 'primaryspeak' which Alexander (1989)[7] calls for, nevertheless it is important to note how holistic the curriculum is thought to be. This is summed up in a quote from one of the infant teachers who shares in the joint summer topic work who said this to me when we were looking at photographs of the children from all four schools happily mixing together and obviously enjoying themselves while working purposefully: 'This what I value most' (pointing to the photographs) 'because education is holistic. I mean, these children are developing socially by mixing with other children and teachers. That has an emotional element too, as does the way they care for one another, and not just from the same school either. Physically, well they are running and jumping and we do dancing together too sometimes. And of course, intellectually, they are learning such a lot on a day like this — so, it's all there isn't it?'

If we take this broader conception of the primary curriculum then perhaps we can accept that small schools, especially when supported in ways such as those described here, may be thought of as rich in educational potential and that supporting them is not about 'counteracting deficiencies' but instead is about 'amplifying opportunities'.

But can these small schools feel positive about the future? All of the Eskdale teachers are extremely anxious at the possibility of losing the Project's support in two years time. They use emotive words like 'bereft' to describe how they would feel to have so much removed that has become an integral part of the way they operate. And yet:

'In respect of such grants, no expectation can be held of them becoming a permanent feature of the rural scene.'[1]

Forward (1988) says:

'The introduction of Educational Support Grants has allowed a number of authorities to set up these large co-operative groups. Whether they will outlast the grant will depend on the value the LEA perceives as arising from this input of financial resource.'[2]

Of course, it is more complicated than this. An authority such as North Yorkshire has many more rural schools who have as yet received no additional funding whatsoever and, despite the value it will undoubtedly feel the Project has been, will not be able to fund at an equivalent level in one geographical area alone, never mind across the whole county. When the teachers are asked to make choices as to what aspects of the Project they feel are the most valuable, they answer unequivocally that all aspects are and refuse to make the choice.

However, that is probably because at present they are not really faced with it. They have two more years of high level, high quality educational support. The most important aspect that I could wish to draw to the attention of those decision-makers who want to know how best to support their small schools is to encourage schools to come together, to foster the development of honest and trusting relationships and to allow them to specify and prioritise their own needs and how these might be met. Then whatever funding is available can be allocated to these schools. Of course, they should have access to information about how other small schools have been supported but it would, I feel, be inappropriate if an authority were to prescribe or impose precise methods of support. For I believe that if trust and autonomy is vested in professional teachers, then such trust will be well rewarded in terms of the worthwhileness of the outcomes for children. For I, unlike some educational decision-makers, have enormous faith and trust in the ability of teachers to use resources at their disposal in the best interests of children. That faith has been well substantiated by the Eskdale Project.

References

1   Bell, A. and Sigsworth, A. (1987) *The Small Rural Primary School*, Falmer Press.
2   Forward, B. (1988) *Teaching in the Smaller School*, Cambridge University Press.
3   Addison, S. (1982) *Small Rural Schools Project 1974-82*, Northamptonshire Education Authority.
4   Campell, R.J. (1985) *Developing the Primary Curriculum*, Holt, Rinehart & Winston.
5   Wilkinson, R. (1989) *A Study of Small Schools' Needs Within the Context of an Educational Support Grant*, B.Ed. (Hons) dissertation, unpublished.
6   Yeomans, R. (1985) 'Are Primary teachers primarily people?' *Education 3–13*, 13(2).
7   Alexander, R.J. (1989) 'Core subjects and Autumn leaves: the National Curriculum and the languages of primary education', *Education 3–13*, 17(1).
8   Alexander, R.J. (1984) *Primary Teaching*, Holt, Rinehart & Winston.
9   Campbell, R.J. (1989) *Junior Education*, Scholastic.

3 Developing a programme in a rural school

Sally Davies

Successful and sustained curriculum development only flourishes within a well organised and managed school. Sally Davies describes how, in the small-scale setting of a rural primary school, effective management strategies can be pursued to bring about positive change.

There are many rural schools across the country and no two are identical. The schools are diverse in their buildings and catchment areas as well as in their styles of internal management, curriculum policies, levels of resourcing and organisation of teaching and learning.

What do rural schools have in common? More than their small size and their country location. The school is often the social and cultural centre of the village. There can be a high level of involvement and commitment from parents and members of the surrounding community which results in a very positive advantage for the school.

In a rural school there may be many reasons for instigating and developing a programme of change. One reason can be the appointment of a new headteacher to the school. This was my experience, and in this chapter I will outline some initiatives, policies and ideas which proved of value in creating movement.

Like many, my first appointment to headship was to a small rural school. It seemed an awesome and challenging task. Previous experience, knowledge and expertise were all needed to prepare for this new role. A newly appointed head brought expectations of change — new ideas, new policies and with these new strategies to bring about developments. The governing body, the teaching staff, parents and children awaited with interest and some apprehension for change to take place. However, should change be based on uncertainty and apprehension? It seemed a far better idea to bring about change through a positive and confident process based on understanding, knowledge and professional judgement leading to the delivery of quality education to all children.

It was important to foster and develop links with parents, governors and the extended community so that there would be a strong unity of purpose and a clear sense of identity. I had no intention of being isolated and alone. There were many new skills to acquire and also there was an acute awareness of the responsibilities of the job. Decision-making, policy planning, curriculum leadership, staff development now happened at my instigation, dependent on my enthusiasm, expertise and ability to bring about change.

On taking up an appointment, though not initially having the competence and confidence which comes through experience, the new head needs rapidly to weigh up the strengths and weaknesses of the school. Learning the basic skills of headship and management of the school have to go hand in hand with revising curriculum and organisation and generating new policies where needed.

Assessing the school

The assessment of the school does not have to be carried out just by the head teacher. To create a more balanced picture, it is of value to ask the staff, however small in number, to contribute in a positive and honest way to this assessment. The local area adviser or inspector can also offer valuable expertise. An inspector who has many isolated small schools to cover may be greatly interested in the plans for the school but is unlikely to find the time to give more than brief general advice and moral support.

A school assessment made in the initial stages of a new headship needs to have structure and clarity of purpose so that everyone involved knows what is taking place and has a positive approach to the exercise. A key factor is the headteacher's willingness to communicate and the headteacher's ability to relate well to everyone engaged in the process of review. Time spent with the staff to increase knowledge and understanding of each other is of paramount importance. Good channels of communication will help reduce anxieties and also hopefully establish a strong working relationship based on joint respect and understanding.

When this assessment is taking place it is helpful to analyse the school under two distinct headings:

a. 'Given' or unalterable variables
b. 'Policy' or alterable variables

The unalterable variables are: buildings, catchment area, staffing levels, physical resources, and rural isolation. The alterable variables are far more complex, they are: style of leadership, school ethos, school organisation, the curriculum, the staff and their professional development, staff responsibilities and parental involvement. There are others that are specific to individual schools.

Out of the review should grow a school policy for the implementation of the National Curriculum and the outline of the school development plan.

Once the school's strengths and weaknesses are identified, then areas can be targeted. To manage change in school, we adopted a simple problem-solving strategy; this clarified the priorities including the in-service training provision (see Figure 1).

Figure 1: A problem–solving strategy

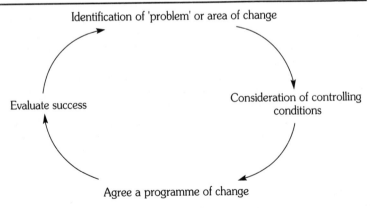

Identifying priorities

There are advantages in managing a small school. With only a few teachers on the staff everyone can become involved quickly and fully in the decision-making process. However, one big disadvantage of the small school is the restricted number of people who can take responsibility for instigating and monitoring change. It is the same few staff who are constantly involved in this process. Most of us are, at times, cautious and even resistant to change. We like where we are and feel secure in what we are doing. Periods of conservatism and resistance to radical change will occur with staff, parents and governors. When asking for change headteachers are often expecting:

a. enthusiasm
b. commitment
c. a willingness to undertake extra responsibility
d. time

When asking people to take a new course of direction and probably to take on more work we need to be sure that we have something to 'trade off' in return — we need to convince a wide variety of audiences that our proposals will lead to a better deal for children.

Once an assessment has been made and areas where change needs to be made have been identified, priorities will need to be established. These will obviously depend on the individual school's needs. It is valuable to look at these priorities at three levels. The first are those that might be achieved in a relatively short time, for example, a review of the general school organisation as far as the management of children before school, at playtimes, at lunchtimes and at the end of the school day. Although not directly linked to curriculum development arrangements such as these are crucial. Children in rural areas often travel relatively long distances to their 'neighbourhood school'. The envelope of care provided by the school needs to be extended to cover the arrangements for the delivery and collection of children if parental approval and support is to be retained and developed. A second level of priorities are those which can be dealt with in the medium term of perhaps a school year. These plans may include change in:

a. classroom organisation and management
b. preparing a curriculum policy statement

c. reviewing job specifications and areas of curriculum responsibility

d. delegating specific responsibility to staff and structuring opportunities for staff development

e. the review at the end of the school year

f. the school's INSET policy

The third level of priorities would be those that would form a five-year plan where the school identifies development which will reflect continuity and most importantly a clear *whole school* approach in which all staff and governors are working together to increase the educational benefits for all the children. This five-year plan also needs to include an annual assessment and review so that modification and adjustments can be made as a result of internal events or as a consequence of directives from the DES.

This structured planning requires a 'vision' of where the headteacher realistically wants the school to be in the future. It requires positive decision-making which reflects the head's ability in the leadership role. The school governing body should be consulted and involved so that there is a clear partnership by all who hold responsibility — a shared agreement.

Managing change

From any assessment of schools it becomes clear that the most important resource of any school is its teachers. Successful change will rely heavily on the attitudes and resourcefulness of the head and through the head to other members of staff. It may not be too difficult to identify areas and policies for change, but success in achieving change will depend greatly on the head's style of leadership. In a small rural school there is the great advantage in that the headteacher will usually have a class teaching responsibility. Therefore strategies and policies for change can be clearly and wholeheartedly demonstrated by possibly 25 %, 33 % or even 50 % of the teaching staff! When opportunities are made for the teaching head to be seen in action by other staff then there is a clear example through practice as well as description.

Effective change relies strongly on how it is managed. Therefore the style of leadership and how the headteacher instigates change will be of fundamental importance. Clear structures of communication are vital, regardless of size of school. The headteacher in search of more than superficial change must be prepared to give time in both formal staff meetings and staff interviews but, if teaching commitment allows, also informally during the working day.

When a policy for change is implemented, e.g. in classroom organisation, there may well be an initial stage of enthusiasm when strategies for change are agreed and implementation is commenced. This can be followed by a difficult stage when progress is not yet evident and doubts are raised.

The headteacher of the small rural school soon becomes well known in the community and is rarely short of well-meaning advice and opinions from parents and the locals as well as the school staff. When changes have yet to bear fruit, continual support and realistic discussion needs to take place. The headteacher must keep up morale, encourage, show consideration, offer expertise and persuasion, because eventually this stage of doubt will pass and time and planning will prove that positive change can be managed successfully. Innovation often demands strength of character, determination, persistence and perhaps even stubbornness from the head.

Curriculum responsibility

To develop a school, its teachers and its curriculum takes time and effort by the headteacher. In rural schools there are few teachers to actually share the load. All teachers, including the head, have to take several areas of the curriculum under their wing. The head must talk to each teacher in turn to assess who can take on responsibility for specific curriculum areas and resourcing.

When these decisions are made and job specifications agreed, the headteacher can plan ways of increasing the expertise and experience of the staff. This is an important aspect of headship; improving staff expertise will benefit the children and the school, and provide greater job satisfaction for teachers. The job specification should include ways in which expertise needs to develop, e.g.:

a. a clearly written brief as to the expectations within the area of responsibility;
b. an entitlement to local authority courses;
c. a responsibility for liaising with colleagues in other schools;
d. visiting schools which clearly demonstrate good practice;
e. an obligation for keeping abreast of developments through the regular reading of books and articles in specific curriculum areas;
f. discussion with the headteacher about opportunities for working alongside other teachers in the school as well as taking responsibility for school-based in-service work.

The explicit statementing of an individual teacher's responsibilities and rights within a three-or four-teacher country backwater is no less vital than carrying out the process in a large urban primary school.

The HMI document *The Curriculum from 5 to 16, Curriculum Matters 2*, states:

> 'A school's curriculum consists of all those activities designed or encouraged within its organisational framework to promote the intellectual, personal, social and physical development of its pupils. It includes not only the formal programme of so-called extra-curricular activities as well as all those features which produce the school's ethos, such as the quality of relationships, the concern for equal opportunity, the values exemplified in the way the school sets about its task and the way in which it is organised and managed.'

This description of the curriculum holds good for all schools, no matter what their size or geographical location.

Staff development

The staff development programme needs to be based on a sound understanding that a school has of its aims, philosophy, ethos and approaches to learning before tackling the specific curriculum areas, because it will be into this context that the curriculum will be disseminated.

We in rural schools are acutely aware of the difficulties in providing the physical and human resources to create and provide a 'broad and balanced curriculum'. One of the ways of easing these difficulties is to tap into the network of external support agencies that may exist in the area. Full use should be made of advisers, advisory teachers, teachers' centres and other colleagues. To help increase expertise it's possible for a small group of rural schools to organise some joint in-service training for their teachers. It helps where the schools involved know each other and have similar expectations, standards and philosophies. This linking together also helps reduce the feeling of isolation which small rural schools can experience. Moyra Bentley, in Chapter 2 of this book, gives examples of ways in which a group of rural schools have collaborated in using advisory teachers to enrich the curriculum. With the increasing demands which are being put on schools, particularly with those relating to the Education Reform Act, the sharing of ideas, plans and policies becomes even more important.

The headteacher has the responsibility to guide policy-making through initial consultation and discussion with the deputy head (if there is one in the small school), and then with the rest of the teachers. Once the general policy direction is decided, then policy documents will need to be written These should clearly reflect the needs of the school and take into consideration the children, the environment, and the aims and the expertise of the staff. In the school assessment previously outlined, decisions will have been reached as to the order of priority for the review and the production of curriculum policies. The timing will be influenced by the National Curriculum and its phased introduction to schools.

A clear plan for the writing of policy documents needs to be implemented. It is important for this responsibility to be under-taken by curriculum leaders as part of their professional development. Overall planning as well as the format of the staff meetings should be a joint decision between curriculum leader and head-teacher. It proves valuable to circulate plans before the meetings so that staff are fully aware of developments.

Even though a headteacher will naturally guide discussions and decision-making on school policies, it is important to struc-ture opportunities for full staff participation, so that staff feel that they have been encouraged to offer their opinion and expertise. Policy decisions can then be made in an atmosphere of confi-dence. Policy statements need to have a sense of belonging to a staff of a school so that they are put into practice as a working document, clearly showing that the theory and practice match. The member of staff involved in the planning can also take the responsibility for minuting the staff meetings, writing out the policy decisions that have been made and, at the conclusion of the programme, shape the curriculum guidelines so that they truly reflect the contributions from all the teaching staff.

Writing and revising curriculum documents is a continuous cycle in the life of a school. New initiatives and priorities require fresh thinking about curriculum content, resourcing and classroom management. Movement of staff and consequent new appoint-ments will also result in change. High standards and expectations will encourage both staff and children to rise to the challenge. The headteacher's expertise must also include the ability to develop and foster a high level of self-esteem in the teaching staff. Teachers only give of their best when they feel confident in themselves and are valued as people both personally and professionally.

All the curriculum guidelines and policy statements which a school makes should effectively influence what goes on in class-rooms. The strength of school policies is the unity of approach which the school develops. In the rural school, it is frequently difficult for the staff to offer expertise across the curriculum. Whereas in a large school it is possible within its organisation to arrange for colleagues with expertise to work alongside other teachers in classrooms, helping to identify objectives, plan the teaching and be engaged in evaluation, small schools do not have this advantage. The headteacher often has a full-time teaching commitment and is unable to personally offer this sort of support or to be able to free teachers to work alongside colleagues in curriculum development. This makes the necessity for full and structured discussion in staff meetings doubly important.

In-service education and training

The INSET programme for the school is an integral part of the school development programme. Releasing members of staff from a rural primary school for courses organised by the LEA often runs into problems that are not experienced in urban areas. Firstly, finding supply cover can be a headache; in rural communities there is rarely a pool of qualified teachers on the doorstep that are seeking supply work. Secondly, getting to a course can involve teachers in travelling considerable distances, making attendance at short 'twilight' sessions impossible. In a large rural county the LEA also faces problems in attempting to provide an adequate number and range of courses to cater for the needs of all its schools.

There should be a continuous programme for training covering the whole of a teacher's professional life from the time of entering college to retirement. The school itself now has to take a far greater role in the training and development of staff than ever before. The school is the agency that can most clearly identify specific needs. Staff development should not only aim to improve current practice and strengths but should also prepare staff for changing responsibilities, enhance job satisfaction and prepare teachers for advancement in their career. Each member of staff will have different professional needs. The head is the co-ordinator and main facilitator for satisfying these needs. In a rural school the staff is a small unit, there may be many demands for increasing staff expertise. As well as school-based in-service, a carefully planned programme of external training is required. This may take the form of attending courses at the teachers' centre, visits to other schools or attending courses organised by colleges or HMI. This expertise and knowledge gained must be disseminated back into the school for the benefit of the other staff. Recording the outlines of school-based in-service work is important, as it indicates where policy changes are taking place and where new responsibilities may lie.

The deputy head of a small rural primary school has special training requirements. There is a need for external training where deputy heads from a number of schools meet to extend their professional development and to share ideas with their peers. In a small school the role of the deputy will in part be different from that of a deputy in a larger school. It is still important that the deputy head is given quality management training which helps in the preparation for future headship. A joint management team is a strong contributory factor in the establishment of a good rural school. Responsibilities need to be delegated, opportunities for leadership offered and sound communication a priority. A deputy needs to know and clearly practice the school's aims and philosophies and compliment the head's management style.

Although school-based in-service is an important part of staff development, it has only been a recent requirement that a school has a systematic and coherent plan for this work. Within this plan should be included opportunities for professional interviews, when staff will have the opportunity to review progress, discuss matters of concern and ways in which careers might be developed. Even within a rural school there will be a need to plan in-service provision on three different levels. Firstly, the whole-school approach when all the staff are involved. Secondly, the in-service training which only a small number of staff would require, e.g. a course on catering for the needs of rising fives in school for the teachers of the infant age children. Thirdly, the provision needed by individual members of staff, perhaps a course on word-processing or an extended course to achieve a Certificate in the Teaching of Primary Science.

Our main aim in all our planning for change through professional development for teachers must be to make a better school for the children.

Philip Gammage, speaking to the National Association for Primary Education, said:

'More recently Kirby — writing on English primary education — said that his book was written about children as individuals whose essential welfare depended upon other individuals. Kirby is writing about relationships. Kirby seems convinced that no matter what the content of the school curricula, no matter how technically proficient teachers are, no matter how good the parent contact, no matter what the academic achievement or level of efficient management, there cannot be a "good" school unless the quality of relationships between all those who work within schools or around them is such that those people draw strength, satisfaction and happiness from them. For Kirby, a good school is about being "good" *with* and *to* people. In our schools we need to consider the value of this statement and to debate the key issue of successful change and its dependence on relationships.'

Finally, we need to assess how effective the policies for change have been and to stand back and review our aims and match them to the reality. Change takes time to consolidate, it needs to evolve and grow from firm foundations. Continual enthusiasm, commitment, reassurance and support is needed from the headteacher, matched with a high expectation for success.

4 Curriculum change and development in an urban school

Brenda Lofthouse

Brenda Lofthouse graphically describes the day-to-day unarmed combat experienced in moving a school forward. Headteachers will identify with the situations she describes and value the solutions proposed.

Much publicity has been given to the establishing of the National Curriculum, and rightly so, but this may have unintentionally obscured an important fact. Curriculum change cannot be implemented effectively without effective school-based curriculum development. School-based curriculum development is as important now as it ever was in the past, and heads of school will, as before, need to be skilful exponents in the arts of management of curricular change in order to implement the National Curriculum successfully, to keep education in schooling, and make the prescribed National Curriculum alive in the imagination of every child.

This chapter is about school-based curriculum development in an urban primary school. This is not meant to infer that the points raised are particular to that type of school. Obviously many skills are common to all types of primary schools, but some skills are directly related to the size and situation of the school. The types of urban school that I have in mind have rolls of between 120 and 250 children with between nine and 12 teaching staff. In

England and Wales, the average size of a primary school is about 180 children. However, it is a fact that urban schools, in the main, have more teaching staff to deploy than rural ones, and this provides urban schools with a crucial advantage. The principles of curricular change are common to all schools; the variable is the number of people involved in the process.

Pre-conditions for successful change: the head

If the change process is to be successful, and not end up as a minor variation in the general direction of the school, then there are certain pre-conditions which should be satisfied. The first set of these concerns the head.

1. The head should have vision of the total curriculum, in terms of content, delivery and ethos. Within this he/she should be goal-oriented so that this vision is achieved through a series of planned objectives. No change can be successfully achieved if it appears to the staff that everything is under attack. Not only does it give negative messages about what the head thinks of the staff through their previous work, but it also means that no one element is properly evaluated for the effects of the change. All plate spinners start by spinning one plate and only start spinning two when they know they can keep both plates moving.

2. Visions are essential but personal. Face-to-face contact to negotiate visions is important, but every head has to allow for variance in effecting that vision. This variance is not necessarily a desire to distort the direction. Everyone interprets things in their own way. Information is filtered through their perceptions into how to achieve the proposed alteration in the curriculum. Knowing this, every goal must be achieved in a series of steps, not just to minimise variance, but to maximize the teaching staff's security in being able to implement the change. If someone is an adherent to Ronald Ridout's method of teaching grammar, it is no use expecting them to change from this to a method whereby the grammar is taught through utilising the child's own writing. Keep using textbooks, but find ones with a better match to the desired outcomes. *The Harpole Report* cites the incident of Pintle going to the

Surplus Apparatus and Staff Illustration Store to put back his Viking longship (made out of 3,500 matches) and claim his Norman castle, it being the season when he 'Did The Normans'. Some teaching methods have been followed by teachers with little variation for a long time as it serves their needs. Curriculum changes frequently alter the balance between teacher needs and children's needs, and in consequence ought to be brought in sensitively.

3. The head must be honest to him/herself as to why he/she wishes to promote the change. It could be:
   a. that he/she wishes to make his/her mark on the school
   b. to impress the local inspectorate
   c. it is something that worked in his/her previous school, went down well with the parents there and so should do well here
   d. it is a change related to the perceived needs of that school.

   Only reason d is a valid reason for change. Improving egos, following bandwagons, or importing previous teaching methods in themselves are not acceptable. It may be the desired change is the introduction of technology in the Early Years, and that the LEA are promoting Early Years Technology, that the head is well versed in it because he/she did a lot of it at their previous school, that he/she introduces it and his/her ego is lifted by the way the children/parents respond. Fine, but these latter factors are incidental to the major requirement for change; that the change is desired because it is related to the head's perception of the needs of the school.

4. Heads should be secure in their judgements. As soon as a head takes over a school, the previous administration has every chance of being accoladed as a golden age — 'When Mr/Mrs Smith/Jones/Brown was here we didn't have bullying/wet knickers/bad weather' etc. etc. It's not true obviously. The message really is 'I knew where I stood with-the-other-one. Now I am not so sure.' Given that, statements harking back in praise of the past both by the staff and parents can be wearying. The same type of thing can happen to a long-serving head who has parts of his/her own past deified: 'It was much better when the school was bigger/smaller/more middling, we had Miss Green/Brown/White here teaching maths/ music/drama' etc.

   No head can please all of the people all of the time; 'the public' are allowed off-days but public people are not. All heads can do is know that the decisions were made with all of the evidence/information available and were taken for the best possible reasons.

To recap. If the head is:

i.   secure in his/her own judgments
ii.   understands that change needs control to effect long-lasting improvements to the curriculum
iii. is sensitive to the threat that change can mean to the security of teachers
iv.   is willing to let veiled comments about predecessors/past events pass him/her by without too much hassle; if these elements are part of the head's understanding of, and reasons for, curriculum change —

then the developments proposed are put forward from a sound basis.

When curricular change in an urban school is envisaged, the head must, before any decisions are made, review the curriculum as it is enacted in totality. The functions of a steam engine cannot be understood merely by completing an intensive study of the smoke-box. Guidelines, if present, should be assessed not only for the concepts presented but also to see how far they have any bearing on the reality of the classroom. How effective is present policy? If staff are going to defend present practice, what practices are they actually protecting? Who is making the curricular decisions? The teacher, the children, the publishers? It was said that there was no need of a National Curriculum whilst we still had dinosaurs and the BBC. What evidence is there of effective learning by children? Are there common strategies for the management of time? Has there been a review of the actual time spent on the various activities the children undertake during a week at school? Has there been a conscious justification for the time spent on activities, or do they exist because they exist? Is the curriculum really broad, and does it have real opportunities for children to develop their thinking? Or is it really elementary in design, with the 3 Rs being used as placebos to curricular breadth, i.e. 'We're doing environmental studies because we are measuring the height of a tree/area of a leaf', etc. All these questions of assessing where we are now have to be answered by the head before any decisions are made regarding curricular change. When all that information is assessed, then judgements can be made as to what changes should be sought. If the review exercise demonstrates that three areas of curriculum need support, discard two of them for the short term.

However dire they may seem, choose only one area for attention. There may well be spin-offs from the selected area, e.g. issues regarding pupils organising their own work/presentation of the work etc., which are applicable to all areas of concern, but changes cannot be properly evaluated if there are too many variables, and valuable lessons will not be learnt from the enterprise. Concentration on one area is important, even with the demands of the attainment targets in the core and foundation subjects as prescribed by the National Curriculum.

As the National Curriculum comes into operation uncertainties are expressed regarding the quantity of content, time available, and the power of decision-making being removed from the teaching profession. There is enough time available for curricular change in urban school. Nobody should feel pressurised into making a quantity of shallow changes in place of quality changes. There is time available for school-based curriculum development strengthening the curriculum where needed, and matching this to the national requirements. Governments cannot legislate for the dynamic relationship of imagination between teacher and child. The power of decision-making in the enactment of the curriculum will always reside with the teacher. The Government might legislate that all children should know about coal mining. One teacher might use textbooks and diagrams, a second build a simulation of mine tunnels with card etc., a third take children to, say, the Big Pit, Abergavenny. All comply with the legislation, but which children will understand most about coal mining?

Never before has school-based curriculum development been more important. For the purposes of the argument it is suggested for a hypothetical urban school that the area which demands revision is science. How can this be wrought?

The Curriculum Development Plan, drawn out in Figure 1, shows the external, school and internal factors which can affect the implementation of change. It is essentially a model for the use of headteachers when considering curricular change. The following part of the chapter is written to highlight different strategies which can be employed, based on a plan of operation as shown.

Curricular change — the noble arts and the black arts

Factors affecting the instigation of change or the pace of change can be internal or external. Obviously national policy can have quite a dramatic impact, but so too, on a local scale, can LEA

Figure 1:   *Curriculum Development Plan* — suggested strategies
for headteachers considering the implementation of curricular
change

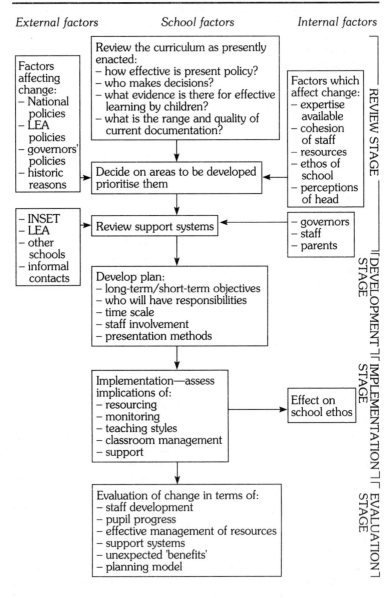

visionaries. Some governing bodies are more aware of curricular issues than others, and can have particular views about the areas under discussion. Sometimes historic reasons affect change. An infant school amalgamated with a junior school may be a 5–11 year primary in name, but have two distinct camps operating within it. External factors can assume great importance where curricular changes do not meet with approval (e.g. William Tyndale) and all these agencies should be respected, but where the noble arts and the black arts of headship most closely fuse is in achieving success by the real adoption of change by the staff of the school.

All curriculum developments have to be planned like a campaign of attack. The advantage should always be with the head because he/she knows it is coming! All effective changes are achieved through consultation and negotiation. Everyone who is affected by the proposals must be party to the decision, have the opportunity to contribute to the proposals. Effective change requires everyone to have ownership of the decisions reached. However, having said that, it is most likely that if the meetings are properly prepared for, the decisions reached are the ones the head is wanting.

Some would describe it as the art of making the head's decisions universalised so that all the staff not only feel ownership over the decision but also believe they thought of it in the first place.

Management of staff: attitudes to change

Changing attitudes is a mammoth task. Headteachers have to be aware that change is threatening and it may well be that the proposed changes in, say, science will have the potential to cause anxiety in some staff who may feel they cannot cope. However there may be others who feel antagonistic towards any demands to review their thinking. They may well have never given any serious consideration as to why they teach science in the way in which they do. It is not that their practice reflects an active awareness of the possibilities and choices available, but rather that it reflects a pathway through that does not tax their working style too much. In a staff of eight to twelve people, one or more members who look upon all change in a negative manner are hard work and have to be planned for. It is possible for a teacher to pursue poor practice but support it as effective by citing some of the results as being what the parents want. To suggest changes whereby the balance of power and control between the teacher and the child alters will not be accepted easily by such a member of staff. In consequence, careful planning for the curriculum staff meeting is essential.

1. The agenda. There should always be an agenda for the meetings and a record should be made of the discussions and decisions taken. Everyone should have access to the agenda, but unless the head knows the staff very well, he/she should avoid extra items being inserted in the agenda without the head's prior knowledge of what issues will be raised by that item.

2. All information, papers etc. which relate to items on the agenda should be circulated well before the meeting and the expectation is that they will be read properly. This way the meeting deals with the issues from a common basis, and valuable time is not wasted in establishing that framework.

3. If the head has a particular proposal, e.g. re-organisation of the science work in school, the arguments for the proposals should be clearly set out in the papers circulated before the meeting which demonstrate all the advantages and possibly any slight disadvantages there might be, and how the changes could be implemented. At the meeting (in a nice, friendly, genial way!) the head should be perfectly honest in stating that this paper is only a framework, a structure set out for discussion, and all the items can be altered or changed, providing that the proposals put forward are better than the ones in the discussion paper. It should be very clearly stated that everything can be changed, and it is best to find small points which are changed to the agreement of all. If the head has done the work properly, put time, thought and energy into the proposals so that the suggested way forward combines the best of present practice with the ideals of good practice, then it is most likely that the proposals will be carried. Even though the staff will have had the papers before the meeting it is extremely unusual for a counter set of proposals to be worked out. Not many people wish to put the time and energy into it that that would demand.

4. Allies. It is far nicer to go into a meeting knowing the audience contains some friends. Usually the head can hope to count on the deputy head as an ally, but this need not always be so. If the deputy head has been acting head, either officially or unofficially, for some period before the arrival of the new head, there can be resentment at the latter's arrival. If the deputy head has been acting head for up to a year, and then been interviewed for the headship and been rejected, there can be outright hostility at the new head's arrival, and an attempt to thwart just about every proposal made. This relationship obviously would have to be worked at and, hopefully

over time, would improve. If the head inherits such a deputy every effort should be made to create a working relationship and sanctuary should not be sought in the belief that the deputy will get a headship soon. Hopefully the deputy is fully supportive of the head and will give any constructive criticism to the head before the meeting. As the staff start to identify with the head's vision of the school it is better that they have the responsibility of carrying proposals through at the meetings. The head and that member of staff work out the proposals beforehand and then that member of staff is responsible for them at the meeting. In this way actual responsibility is given to the postholders, together with the proposals for change coming from within the staff as well as from the head. The head can then give total backing to the proposals, but the thrust for change comes from two sources. The head should not believe that they alone have all the answers to all the questions. Acknowledgement of others' expertise should be high on the agenda. If the staff/head relationships develop well, the head, having set the framework, should then be able to achieve the role of 'thrust co-ordinator', so that the developments are worked at in turn by those with the expertise; the power of the head is not diminished by the staff with this development. Rather it is the head enabling the staff to develop professionally which actually increases the effective power of the head.

5.   Blockers. These delightful pieces of behaviour are followed by staff members determined to sabotage team efforts. There are seven common ways in which sabotage can be attempted:

-   blocking: being negative, trying to rework the agenda
-   attacking: deflating the status of others
-   being playful: displaying lack of involvement in the team's efforts
-   recognition seeking: boasting about previous achievements to prevent being placed in an inferior position
-   deserting: doing tasks unrelated to the team's function and goals
-   pleading special interests; speaking for 'my class', 'the parents' etc., usually to cloak one's own prejudices
-   dominating: attempting to manipulate others in the team.

If you are the head and you are faced with any or all of these attempts to thwart the achievement of the objectives set it can be an unpleasant experience. At one staff meeting one member of staff decided to test my vocabulary with sentences like, 'Did I see the County initiative in the context of a ukase?' Only two days before I had looked up the word 'ukase' as I did not know what it meant. However I dealt with the question as if ukase and I were on very familiar terms, and the staff member stopped playing that game. (This was fortunate for me for the chances of them choosing a word I did not know were quite high.) Looking at watches whilst the proposals are put forward, citing potential disaster areas, talking to the member of staff next to them whilst others are talking, these and other far more obvious hostilities can be wearying. Strategies in dealing with them vary in directness, but such a situation should never be allowed to develop into an argument where one side is forced to lose face. Neither side can afford that. The head certainly can't as he/she is on show and the leadership skills they demonstrate in this situation will, to a large extent, determine the allegiances which are formed in relation to future proposals. The negative staff can't lose face as they are performing in front of their colleagues and they will have spoken at length to them before the meeting about how nothing on earth would get them to agree to x, y, and z! A divided staff offers another power base and should be avoided at all costs. Deal with the aggression in as relaxed manner as possible. Dollops of humour are important. Gradually and subtly seek to isolate the negative staff so that it can appear that these negative attitudes are against the general will of the meeting. This member of staff is not then just fighting the head, but also the majority of his/her colleagues. The head should take from the arguments something which can be incorporated into the main plan, show generosity, but never lose control of the meeting. Where ever possible, the head should achieve saying 'no' by going through a loop of yes ... but! This way nobody has their effort rejected, they do not face humiliation, and they remain comfortable at the meeting and are willing to contribute again. Hopefully the desire to pursue blocking tactics will lessen as time passes, the cohesion of staff relationships improves, previous successes will encourage future successes and the atmosphere is good for all concerned. However if a member of staff actively seeks to thwart the head and is openly antagonistic to the head's leadership then the head has to take matters to the notice of people outside of the school, the LEA and the governors, and it may eventually result in that member of staff facing disciplinary action. This should not be entered into unless all other possibilities have been tried, but all staff members, regardless of their opinions, have a duty to act professionally. The head should never duck difficult decisions.

Developing the plan

Assuming that the staff are all in agreement about the necessity for change, there should be a plan developed so that the way ahead is clear. The suggestion outlined in Figure 2 is a plan to develop science in relation to the requirements of the National Curriculum in a nursery and primary school which has 10 members of staff. The assumptions are that two people on the staff have a good science background and that all of the staff are used to working well together for the benefit of the curriculum for the children.

Figure 2: Outline development plan for science in the National Curriculum

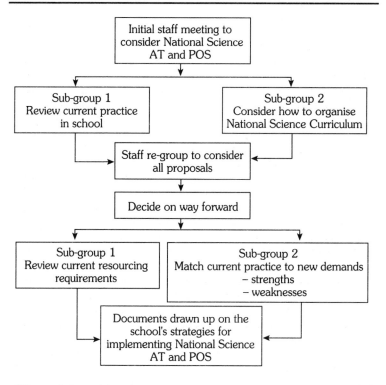

AT — attainment target
POS — programme of study

From such a development plan long-term and short-term objectives are implied. The short-term ones are actually organising a strategy, to which all the staff contribute, which will enable the school to provide pupils with the relevant experiences. Decisions will have to be made about which experiences the nursery children will have. The National Curriculum does not encompass them, but there are implications for them in that certain expectations are made of the five-year-old, e.g. can sort by colour, shape, etc., so the nursery children should be taught colours, basic shapes etc. Long-term objectives involve the re-assessment of the strategies in the light of successive evaluations of practice.

Initial meetings, which all staff attend, assess the content of the science document. Everyone must be familiar with the proposals in order to make informed judgments as to how the school should develop its science programme. If a head has built a highly motivated team, a high performing team, the members of staff will co-operate well with one another as success is seen as recognition of the whole school, not of any one individual. As these teams develop the head's leadership role changes to meet the new situations. As the staff team performance increases and higher targets are met, the head's role does not lose the functions involved in curriculum intervention and setting standards but it increasingly takes on a linking role, ensuring that everyone is listened to and involved. Heads should seek ways of delegating responsibilities in order to create time for themselves to concentrate on tasks which are required of them, but more importantly, so that they are able to nurture the professional development of their members of staff.

From the initial meetings it should be decided what needs doing and who is going to do it. It should be decided what level of commitment will be needed and how the information gained will be presented. Factors affecting this include secretarial time etc. which may be involved. It is suggested that the staff divide into two groups to review past practice and future requirements. These groups should be balanced in terms of experience, expertise, and the roles people will adopt (sometimes known as advisers, organisers, controllers and explorers). From the plan in Figure 2, sub-group 2 might decide that the science curriculum should be organised into topics, and they select the following areas:

1. Sounds and music
2. Ecology
3. Planet earth
4. Weather
5. Human biology
6. Animal and plant life
7. Structures and forces

When the staff re-group it may well be that the topics suggested are agreed by all, but 7, 'Structures and forces', is at present most under-represented in the school's curriculum. What support can the school seek?

INSET

Many of the INSET courses provided over the past few years have been concerned with the process as opposed to the product. The demands of the National Curriculum may change the nature of in-service courses to become far more content-based in order to give teachers the skills and knowledge they require. A number of reports from the 1978 Primary Survey onwards have commented upon the lack of consistency in science teaching in primary schools. The National Curriculum is seeking to eradicate that. However, given that at present everyone is adjusting to the new demands, the staff may not find the answers to their particular queries in the form of established INSET courses. It is likely to be more beneficial to run school-based INSET curriculum development meetings by inviting into the school members of the Inspectorate, members of the subject-based advisory teams, staff from colleges etc., or to join with other schools facing the same problem and have joint sessions. In this way the identified problem can be specifically addressed, rather than possibly just touched on in a pre-set INSET course. There is nothing more frustrating than to have one's awareness of a problem raised by a speaker when one is already aware of the issue. It is not, however, reasonable to expect answers in the manner of finding the Holy Grail to AT 5. As ever, there is no one right answer. The school staff must discuss all the issues, and with the information they have gained, seek to provide the best solution they can for the children in their school. However the information gained from providers will be better if they have been given a clear brief as to the nature of the problems and time to address themselves to the solution. An 'in-house' provider, e.g. Inspectorate, member of advisory team, can be useful in that they should have access to all the initiatives being carried out in the whole County.

Resources

Assuming the development plan has been followed, information gained, and the topics agreed, Topic 7 (above) might be written up as in Figure 3 in terms of initial description.

Figure 3: Topic 7: structures and forces

Attainment Target(AT)	Level	Statement	Activity	Resources
4	1	1	Investigation of physical properties of as wide a range of materials as possible	Basic materials kit containing, for example, natural sponge, dough, synthetic sponge, plasticene, rubber (hard and soft), polystyrene (hard & soft), plastic (hard & soft), packaging, cling film, wood — sawdust, shavings, chips, balsa — cork (hard & soft), fabrics (natural & man-made), fibres (raw & woven), metals, tins, foil, paper clips, range of metal discs, marble, shells, paper, glass, mirror, perspex.

Staff decisions will have to be made as to how the resources are to be assembled. Are they to be gleaned from friendly sources? Are they to be bought in from manufacturers? How are they to be stored, centrally or in each classroom or both? Who is to be responsible for ensuring that there is a plentiful supply? These basic management questions concerning the distribution of resources have to be decided by the whole staff. Good storage facilities are vital and it may be that initially as much money is allocated to this as to the resources they are to contain. The staff must decide on the documentation that is required. How will the resources be listed? What evaluation will be carried out, not just of the progress the children are making, but of the programme itself? Has sufficient money been allocated to the science curriculum? Given that some sponsored events raise money more easily than others, should there be a sponsored event to raise money for additional computer equipment, and spend money allocated for that technology on resourcing a materials kit? What evaluation will be made of the teaching strategies and the total approach to classroom management? For this last evaluation to be effective there must be real trust between the staff. Evaluation of others' successes and failures is far easier to undertake than an evaluation of one's own successes and failures. Yet it must be done as in-class help and support may be essential in the early stages of implementing a new programme. One important part of the evaluation procedure will be to assess how much of the school's time and energy is going into promoting the core subject, and whether this is to the detriment of the other parts of the curriculum.

Finally, it is the head's job to ensure as far as it is possible that all the curricular changes that are achieved promote staff cohesion, not staff disintegration. The needs of the children are frequently voiced, but the needs of the staff are just as important. Teachers need recognition of their efforts. They need praise, interest, encouragement and support. If the school has been recognised in some way by someone speaking well of it, all the staff should be told of this at a staff meeting. Success begets success. The staff's personal needs should be understood, as should their professional needs. All staff have a right to an objective review of their progress during the past year, and to the setting of new goals and objectives. People need to develop new horizons, for the wider their personal horizons the better informed their vision for the children will be. Part of the goal-setting should be being given new and real responsibilities. If the staff are developing their professional responsibilities they should be encouraged to experiment, and excel. They may well excel at areas which go beyond the head's expertise. There is no threat in this for the head if the framework is set whereby the higher our achievements the better the school. The staff should work at collective problem-solving, be it a difficult child, a time issue or whatever. In this way cohesion and continuity of philosophy is achieved and the children understand much more clearly the framework in which they work. School staff should avoid becoming too insular. It is quite easy to become enmeshed in one's own school issues and not relate to other schools at all. Time should be set aside for making opportunities to see other people at work within one's own school and for seeing other teachers at work in their own schools. When selecting other schools it is worth going to 'well-known' schools and less well-known ones in terms of local repute. There is a lot of good work going on in a wide variety of schools. Staff should see real teachers teaching real children, but in order to make the most out of the time available, discussion should precede the visit so that the staff have clear objectives of what they are looking for.

After each visit there should be a de-briefing session of what was seen. Finally the staff should be encouraged to read books relating to educational practice, or at the very least take the TES each week!

In conclusion, long-lasting changes can be achieved in schools by the head taking the initiative and seeking to develop expertise in the staff. The head should not lose sight of the total vision of what he/she wants the school to achieve, but should always remember that the school belongs to everyone. No head should think of it as 'my school'. It is the centre of the working lives of a lot of people. The *gestalt* is bigger than the sum of its parts. Good leadership recognises what others can do well, and seeks to develop in those who are not as competent, greater abilities. Yet for all that, the job of the head can be a lonely one. Praise falleth from the heavens, and rarely seems to raiseth, unless the head has a good secretary, often worth their weight in gold!

References

'Influencing and Supporting Staff Development in the context of the National Curriculum', handout given at Primary Heads' Course, Stoke Rochford, Feb.1989
Carr, J.L. 1972 *The Harpole Report* Secker and Warburg, London

Acknowledgement

Thanks to Colin Richards for advice offered.

5 Consultancy in the primary school

David Winkley

The traditional role of the LEA Inspector/Adviser is rapidly changing. The inspectorial aspect now dominates with little time being available for pastoral responsibilities. Schools are faced with increasing demands for efficiency and effectiveness and are faced with new responsibilities through Local Management of Schools. New avenues of professional support need to be identified or schools are likely to find themselves floundering.

In this chapter David Winkley makes the case for an imaginative use by schools of consultants drawn from a variety of backgrounds to investigate teaching, resourcing, children's achievement and general management so that issues are illuminated from a variety of perspectives. He convincingly argues that, on the basis of these investigations, informed decisions on forward planning can best be made.

The new post-Reform Bill world seems likely to encourage new markets for advisory and consultancy support. Schools as institutions can do a great deal to help themselves, and the logic of the current rapidly changing education scene will surely promote more groundfloor initiatives. Advisers have traditionally offered help, but their complex relationship to central management and their inspectorial and promotional control role can compromise their potential as consultants. For the *sine qua non* of consultancy is that it's on the client's terms.

But whom do you invite in to help and for what reason? There are plenty of people in the educational business (and outside it) who may well have something to contribute in managing change. We might begin by questioning the assumption that the activity of consultancy lies like a polar star 'out there', a specialist expertise beyond the reach of most of us. In fact consultancy is fundamentally a mode of teaching, admittedly of a very particular kind, focused very often on the development of groups or whole institutions, but calling for many of the general qualities which characterise interactions between all good teachers and learners. As Christopher Dare puts it:

> 'It is difficult to envisage a definition of consultation that marks the activity as totally distinct from that of the teacher.'[1]

Effective teaching, like effective consultancy, depends on the quality of interaction between teacher and learner. It follows that all teachers are in some measure 'consultants'. I see my own daily work with teachers and children as having a consultancy dimension. The familiar gambit rings in your head — setting up the role of the responsive consultant:

> 'Please sir can I have a word with you...'
> 'I wonder if you've got a minute or two...'
> 'There's a problem here, I wonder if...'

Teachers should see part of their work as acting as consultants, to children, parents and to their own colleagues.

Consultants, then, ought to fit naturally into the everyday process of school life. As in all learning situations, the way to success is to persuade learners that this is the way to do it, this maybe is the way forward, this may crack the problem, and that they (as learners) have the strength to make progress for themselves. The teacher helps, advises, informs, feeds back but does not substitute. The aim is to free the learner from the constraints of support so that he/she can take the initiative on for him/herself. The key role of the teacher is leading the learner towards insight.

If we take this very wide view of consultancy as a constituent part of the learning process we begin to see both its importance and its limitations. Its importance lies in the likelihood that advisers and consultants are at the heart of the learning process and not merely peripheral to it. Its limitations lie in the fact that all learning in the end has to be grasped and taken on by the learner himself. Useful consultancy is not brash, managerial, directive, or controlling. Nor, by and large, is it concerned with providing simple solutions to obvious problems (of the kind which can be largely self-identified). It calls for self-confidence, a sound knowledge base, highly developed antennae for appreciating the learning needs of others, and considerable personal skills. It calls for a strange combination of the knowledgeable, confident and self-effacing. Elsewhere I have described the consultant as like the young Victorian lady — well informed and talented, but waiting to be asked.[2]

Adults are no different in the broad range of their learning needs from children. Groups of staff need help and advice, as do individuals. It follows that

> 'There is ... no conceptual difference or clash between our approach in understanding an individual, a couple, a family, a group or an institution'[3]

— though there will be many different skills and methods called for in supporting different kinds of interaction.

Consultant help can come from inside or outside the school. Many primary teachers are now expected to take on a consultancy role in particular curriculum areas, and my own school, like most others, has internal expertise on offer in a range of specialist areas. It follows that it is useful for primary teachers to study the consultancy process and to consider how it might work most effectively in their own idiosyncratic situations.

Of course, the brief of an internal postholder, like an adviser's, may be partly managerial and mandatory, where staff are expected to listen and to respond. There is inevitably the potential for tension and conflict here. It is unfortunately true that some learning comes about by our being forced into difficult, new, or demanding situations. The external consultant starts off from a different perspective by virtue of the fact that he is there entirely at the behest of the client. In practice, differences between insiders and outsiders may become less clear, partly because the clever postholder manages to turn a managerial task into a consultancy one by persuading the staff that what needs to be done is worth doing co-operatively; but partly because all creative learning tends to develop through a tension between established ideas and the threat of the new. And all consultants touch upon the struggle to change. The teacher, staff group or whole institution that resists the challenge will have great difficulties in gaining the kind of insight that leads to change. It follows conversely that the client needs to be open to risk, difficulty and perhaps a little pain in coming to terms with close scrutiny if progress is to be made.

The challenge then is similar for internal and external consultants, though McLean[4] argues convincingly that there are often advantages in using outsiders. It is the external consultant who can bring the new perspective, the detached view, in a way that is difficult for an insider closely drawn into the private theatre of his particular world. The outsider is like an audience, seeing the play in a fresh way.

The theory of consultancy

It helps in understanding consultancy to think of it in relation to a simple structure of three broad areas of reference. Each can be applied at different levels, ranging from the whole school to the individual classroom.

1. Management

There is a well established tradition of management consultancy more developed in industry than in most other areas of public life.

There are many functional elements of the management of school life which can be usefully detailed. An analysis may look across the whole school at such issues as the use of time, personnel, general running procedures, questions of efficiency. On a smaller scale management procedures in classrooms can be examined, and here there are a host of questions to ask about how children, resources, classroom procedures are managed. Everard gives a number of interesting examples of the involvement of consultants in the analysis of the aspects of school management — sometimes using industrial expertise. He argues that:

> 'there are numerous examples of teachers' efforts being inefficiently applied and needlessly dissipated, where it would appear that no-one has stood back to review the way in which work (especially of an administrative nature) is done, whether in fact it is worth doing at all ....'[5]

There is no shortage of examples of management consultancy in action. Some of these describe general approaches to improving the consciousness and insight of management teams, usually using problem-solving techniques and systematic group work. But there are many detailed aspects of school life which consultants have (and might) illuminate. They tend to be problem-oriented. Morris [6] for example, anatomises in detail a case of a school having problems with meetings. Most of these examples tend to focus on larger schools (usually secondary). But the development of local school management will undoubtedly sharpen the need to look more precisely at the efficient use of time, effective ways of managing finance and administrative activity in ways that don't undermine professional energy and initiative. Schools, including smaller primary schools, will need to look at effective ways of holding together the increasingly complex involvements of governors, head and staff in school development. Outside advice and support may well be essential in all this.

2. Curriculum

There are numerous interesting examples of curriculum consultancy in action. Most LEAs have a cohort of teacher-advisers and subject specialist advisers who assist in a variety of ways in the development of school curriculum. Teacher advisers have made a particularly active contribution here both in supervising teacher activity in school, and in initiating and supporting projects over long periods of time. The quality of such consultancy is often very high, as with the widely acclaimed National Writing Project which involved consultants working in classrooms to support teachers' own initiatives, and showing teachers ways in which to develop their consultancy skills to *pupils*.

There will be interesting opportunities in the future to look at new questions of the *timing* of elements of curriculum — once the national curriculum is in place — and to work out balances between curriculum elements, examining the quality of the tasks children undertake, and how learners can make an active contribution to their own learning, even within a pre-ordained curriculum programme. The developing field of action research will have a role in all this, with teachers working with higher education tutors in examining each other's practice in detail.

3. Personnel

The focus here is on the personal needs of individuals or groups, their feelings, confidence, abilities, problems. The consultant concerned with this area (as all good consultants will be in some degree) will take a concerned view of the impact of management and curriculum decisions on participants. Industrial consultancy over the years has increasingly become concerned with people's attitudes and feelings. Experiential learning on management courses, as Everard describes it[7] leads to much greater awareness of 'interpersonal and intergroup processes, which in turn means that the participants are able to tackle new problems more systematically than before'. There is a clear link between personal insight, people's feelings and motivations and wider issues of management delivery. And there is clear evidence that harmonious and creative working together of teachers in groups is one of the key components in effective schooling.[8]

There are a variety of ways in which consultancy can help in focusing on people's feelings and personal needs in schools. Teachers have the right to expect effective consultant support from senior staff — and the head in particular — and there is considerable skill in developing professional and appropriate supports to teachers with different needs. Advisers have tended to take on a consultancy role with headteachers, though this is often unsystematic and superficial. Formal appraisal schemes may in the long run encourage more systematic use of consultancy support for all teachers, though appraisal must not be confused with consultant support. Children also have a right to personal support. It has probably been children with special needs who have been most effectively served in the past through access to the educational psychologist, or (even better) a sensitive teacher who can listen and respond in a supportive, sustained and imaginative way. My own school has a trained teacher-counsellor who is available to discuss any child's personal needs on request.[9]

There are also examples of teacher groups supported by outside consultants. These may prove increasingly useful in the future, especially in schools with high rates of stress. This group of teachers was supported by a consultant psychiatrist:

> 'The group of seven teachers and the consultant met once a fortnight and the teachers took time in presenting a detailed description of an individual child. Everyone was encouraged to come with their thoughts and observations and gradually a clearer picture built up of the child, his family, his situation and his present functioning. It is often very useful to think about how the teacher and other children feel towards the child and to try to sort out what are the teacher's own feelings and what feelings the child induces in the teacher or other children through his behaviour.'[10]

Such group discussion can act as a support to the teacher as well as giving the teacher insight into their own and each other's feelings. Wittenberg[11] describes similar work with teachers in London.

There are a variety of personnel issues, some trivial, some profound, that may benefit from systematic examination and support in the day-to-day life of a school. Support will be based upon recognising the enormous importance of 'feelings' in schools between staff, between staff and children, and in the children themselves.

The brief

'The consultant cannot carry out the task of consultation without being aware of the contract that is being set up between the consultee or consultees and the consultant.'[12]

The consultant, like an advocate, needs a brief. The precise criteria of this brief need to be negotiated with the school, with all participants involved in the exercise — the classteachers, the headteacher, and in some circumstances, the parents and the governors. There are a number of things to be considered:

- we need to be clear why we've brought someone in from outside to help us.
- we need to know what the consultant has to offer.
- we need to make it clear in what way we think he/she will be able to help us.
- we need to be precise about the focus of the involvement — on management, curriculum, personnel development, or some combination of all three.
- how long will the consultancy last? Is it a short-term involvement, or will it last a term or longer?
- what kind of access does the consultant have to the school? Completely open or (say) certain times during the week with (perhaps) a limited number of classes and teachers and children?
- what is the role of consultant? Is it to inform (e.g. via lectures or practical sessions), or is it to *observe* and monitor and feed back evidence?
- what kind of reporting back is expected? Is it to be written, and if so how long is the report expected to be? Will there be any opportunity for discussion, and if so will this be formal or informal or both? And who will have access to the information, written or otherwise?
- what plans are there to respond to the outcomes of the consultant's involvement?

We now need to consider, as part of this brief, the different ways in which the consultant can become involved in the school, first in terms of the *stages* of involvement in change — at the beginning, middle or end stages; and second in relation to the relative *depth* of involvement in the school life.

Stages of involvement

The consultant may become involved at a variety of different *stages* in development. These may broadly be divided into three categories:

1. Involvement in the early stages of a project or development. This may require involvement in initial planning, in supporting conceptual development as well as in the experimental or piloting stages of an initiative.
2. Involvement in supporting or monitoring the *progress* of an established on-going initiative. One school, for example, brought in a consultant after setting up a new maths scheme: the consultant was not involved in the choice or initial stages of the development of the scheme, but the school wanted some feedback once they had the initiative on the go to see whether progress was on the right lines.
3. Assessment of some aspect of the school which is well developed and in a relatively *finished* form.

The consultant, then, may be involved in any one or in all of these 'developmental' stages, but must recognise that the nature of involvement will be very different at the different stages.

Depth of involvement

Next, there is the question of the depth of involvement of the consultant in the life of the school. Is his/her work likely to be a narrow strand of activity closely focused on a highly specific task? Or is it to be general, concerned with the general running, ethos and nature of the school?

The issue of generality

The difference in consultancy between looking at the 'whole-school context' and looking at bits and pieces of it — at one curriculum strand for instance — has been long recognised in the structuring of the LEA advisory services [13] in which distinctions have been evolved over the years between the curriculum specialist adviser and the 'general adviser or inspector'. There has been increasing pressure on advisers to act as consultants to teachers whilst also monitoring and inspecting schools according to LEA requirements, though it is hard to find convincing examples of a satisfactory LEA advisory structure which at the end of the day offers a wide range of consultancy services in the different areas of management, curriculum and personnel development, and also meets central LEA management requirements.

The specialist-generalist problem which has traditionally faced advisory services needs facing at school level.

The first consideration for the school is whether and to what degree it wants the consultant to consider issues concerning the running of the whole school. Such a 'review' or 'inspection' or broad process of discovery or description is likely to be demanding in time, needing a high level of organisation and diplomacy.

At the moment it is relatively rare for schools to appoint external consultants to engage in whole school reviews. This is usually seen as the province of LEA advisers (often acting in an inspectorial rather than a consultancy role) but there is every possibility that schools will increasingly want to appoint their own external assessors. The devolution of funding to schools, the pressures for performance review and the strategic interests of governors will hasten such developments.

We may face issues here that have bedevilled inspection at LEA and HMI level since its evolution over the years from amateur detective work to professional reportage, and the story is by no means over yet; the problems of whole-school review are far from resolved. A complete spring cleaning of every corner of school life, reported in detail and in writing is useful in giving a general overview of progress, or if you want to identify cans of worms (such as the school that kept its art stock in the PE showers) — but is a hugely expensive and cumbersome business which suffers not only from problems of time and expense but tends to go rapidly out of date. The HMI school inspection programme sometimes throws up interesting information to LEAs, and gives useful insights into individual schools: but most schools only have a full inspection once in a blue moon, and arguably the LEA ought not to need the ponderous hand of central government to audit individual institutions. Central information-gathering for research, or wide LEA analysis (of the kind HMI undertake) is another thing altogether.

On the other hand, schools might engage in self-review more systematically using the currency and knowledge of LEA advisers and HMI to support increased independence and self-reliance in such matters.

The line of analysis which seems most productive is what is sometimes called by inspectors 'dipstick' review and it's interesting to give an example:

> 'I wanted, as headteacher, to carry out a developmental programme in the school. I had my own view, of course, of the school's strengths and weaknesses in different areas, but such is the complexity of school life I need my views confirmed (or disconfirmed) at different points in my analysis. Moreover I wanted a wide-arching picture of the whole school before the staff spent time and effort over the next year on particular issues. I wanted above all supporting evidence for our sense of priorities. So did the school staff, and — at more of an arm's distance — the school governors. The case for the involvement of a perceptive outsider involved in the exercise was overwhelming.'

The most practical way in which this might be done is the 'plumbline' or 'dipstick' approach. This would provide a general overview of the school, followed by a narrower, more specific focus on particular problem areas.

'Dipstick' consultancy calls for the consultant as part of his brief to examine broad links between the management of the school, curriculum development and delivery and personnel and relationship issues. It focuses on a relatively narrow series of items by examining their development and implementation across boundaries.

The fascinating story of the development of a particular theme through the school can be enormously revealing and can carry us into deep waters. Small revelations can carry wide implications.

An effective dipstick consultancy might, therefore, take a topic chosen by the school as important in its current priorities. It would examine its historical evolution in the school. It would consider aspects of management and planning, efficiency, procedures, meetings, communications, documentation, time spent. It would look at curriculum foundation and classroom delivery. It would consider questions of quality and (if it was a curriculum area its cross-curriculum links) and would then try to locate its relation to personnel issues (quality of motivation, skills of teachers, reactions of learners, its place within the wider ethos of the school). It would come to a view of the relation between the key areas of management, curriculum and personnel, the complexity of links and points of strength and weakness.

Consultancy in action

Suppose, for example, the school took on the relatively straightforward task of improving its work in pottery. The most effective approach might begin with a dipstick review of the school's current practice in art work, or (if the brief was narrowed) in pottery itself.

The initial review would require the following:

1. a survey of the current management and planning processes in the development of pottery. Do staff meet, when, how do they inform each other, make decisions, monitor progress etc.?
2. resources, their nature, planning and usage;
3. links between pottery and other art activities;
4. quality of practice in a number of different classrooms;
5. links between pottery/art and other curriculum areas;
6. sequencing of practice throughout the school;
7. insight into the attitudes and state of knowledge of staff;
8. processes of assessment and display;
9. quality of achievement.

The focus on pottery, however specific, would bring out a good many general issues. It will reveal a good deal about the school's planning and management process, the ability of staff to work together, the quality of implementation and the variability of the staff, the school's assessment procedures (or lack of them).

A full and effective analysis will need judgement not only of general planning issues at school and classroom level, about time and organisation, and may even carry the school's thinking into deeper theoretical issues about (say) the tension between focus on skills and the focus on personal satisfaction in the experience of pottery. How much do achievements and finished products matter, how much is the 'process' or hands-on experience the key issue? Issues involving people's feelings and beliefs may well be drawn in here. Mrs X thinks sequential skills leading to high quality products ought to be the main focus. Mr Y profoundly disagrees. What counts for him is 'play experience' which leads (he believes) to better long-term imaginative engagement of the children with clay. Mrs X children's work on the other hand is well presented, fired in a kiln, varnished and finished. Mr Y's children don't produce a lot but enjoy their play activity with clay and the teacher generates a lot of enthusiasm. These kinds of observation have implications for whole school life, focusing widely on the nature of curriculum delivery, classroom management, and child experience. All this might come out of a dipstick analysis.

A 'general' overview of this kind illuminates the school's inner workings. The fact that such research is focused will make it all

the more useful for the school. This school, concerned to develop
its pottery, can now consider:

- the question of skills versus 'play' as a philosophical question;
- questions of how much time classes spend on pottery;
- questions of how to set up policy-making sessions and decision-making procedures so that all the staff agree to do more pottery;
- ideas for encouraging children to 'have a go' at pottery.
- planned opportunities for Mrs X, the most experienced teacher, to help less confident members of staff;
- reassessment of resources for art;
- how to improve support and mutual respect between staff;
- how to generalise the planning and support processes for the development of pottery into other curriculum areas;
- how to develop a regular review of achievement and progress in pottery.

The issues for management were:

– more money needs to be allocated to clay, and the clay needs
looking after better. Twenty-five per cent was wasted. The head
and staff need to look at more effective ways of planning and
evaluating their art activities. The art postholder needs to be
more specific in setting tasks. The head needs to be more aware
of the staff dynamics and plan formally for resolution of the
problems between Mrs X and Mr Y. There needs to be a better
flow of communications between all staff, and formal planning
arrangements for the arts curriculum generally needs devising.

The curriculum issues were:

– the whole staff needs to think in more depth about art curriculum. The staff need to plan their time better in the classroom
to allow more balance between two and three dimensional art.
The staff need to look at more efficient uses of time — at ways in
which pottery activity can be more clearly integrated.

The personnel issues were:

– that the dynamics on the staff are undermining clear professional thinking. Staff are insufficiently supportive to each other.
The outstanding practitioner is not having sufficient opportunity
to support other staff. Mr Y, whose dislike of Mrs X is irrational,

needs counselling. Opportunities for resolving and debating philosophical issues need planning. There needs to be more value given to the achievements of Mrs X. The staff group as a whole needs to be given more support and opportunity to work together.

This analysis has brought up problems, described aspects of how the school works, has picked up philosophical tensions and a sense of the school's dynamics. It has shown strengths and weaknesses in achievements. It shows too, how the different strands interconnect.

All this is very useful, but doesn't in itself, of course, solve the school's problems. It accurately highlights the issues, but it's now up to the school to tackle them.

A close analysis of this kind cuts deeply into the texture of the school, giving insight, a bird's-eye view; but now the school may need to draw on other kinds of advice to help resolve some of the particular issues raised.

The school might, for example, arrange a series of practical sessions on how to teach pottery at various ability levels, bringing in a local teacher of pottery to do this. It might be useful to have an input from a school head who has experience of staff development, who can describe in detail how he tackled the management of curriculum in his own school. It might be useful to have someone from outside to support the less confident members of staff in the classroom. It might be useful to bring in outside support from (say) art students to work at pottery skills with groups of children. The school might consider an artist in residence. It might implement a three-dimensional artwork competition, and bring in someone to assess the artwork at the end of the year. The school might call upon an adviser to counsel Mrs X and Mr Y., though in the first place this ought to be a priority for the head. It might draw on a consultant to help them steer a new art curriculum through its difficult early stages. And when the new curriculum programme is running well, it may consider another consultant to come and review the progress of the 'programme in action'.

We begin to see the range of possibilities for a school in developing further outside contacts. I have at my own school made use of the following:

- lecturers who give insight
- teachers who demonstrate their skills and run practical sessions for staff
- outside consultants to give advice in the early stage of developing projects

- dipstick analysis of specific curriculum areas
- performance review consultants, who come in to assess the way a particular curriculum programme is going.

On one occasion six consultants were invited by the staff to analyse the school 'project' curriculum in science, environmental studies, history, geography, health, and RE. There was a GP, a university lecturer, a college lecturer, and three LEA advisers. Each contributed a detailed analysis, produced a lengthy written report and discussed their views in a written report. The 'brief' extended an open invitation to each consultant to visit the school at any time over the period of a term, to spend time in classrooms, to examine the children's work, to assess the children before and after the project programme, orally or in writing (if they chose).

The outcome was a series of reports which moved the thinking of the school forward, addressed itself to teaching skills, to resourcing, to children's achievement and to questions of planning and wider questions of achievement appropriateness and success in what the teachers planned and executed. The reports were practical, thoughtful, but hardnosed and often critical.[14] The teachers, after an initial nervousness, were wholly appreciative of the experience.

But what struck us most of all was the professionalism of the various consultants we called upon, and this raises the question of skills and qualities called for in consultancy.

The qualities of consultants

The uses of consultancy are enormously varied. It follows that schools can make use of a variety of different kinds of skills. Three questions that any consultant has to ask are:

1. what am I good at?
2. what have I got to offer that is useful?
3. how can I best respond to the client's needs?

There are aspects of consultancy that call for very specific knowledge-based skills. Who is interested in a mathematics INSET session run by someone who is not experienced and knowledgeable in the teaching of maths? As with all teaching, quality of communication is vital, and you expect the consultant to be a clear, relevant and lively communicator.

But the more complex the consultancy, the more the consultant is likely:

a.   to dipstick — to consider wide issues of school management and ethos;
b.   to deal with people at length and in depth;
c.   to face issues of internal school politics;
d.   to stay longer in the school;
e.   to develop a more sustained analysis of the school;
f.   to become involved in the processes of the long-term development of some dimension of the school.

For such activities, special skills are required, particularly in handling people. Consultants who are insecure, brash or overweeningly self-confident are likely to undermine their own credibility. Warmth, sensitivity and diplomacy are pre-conditions of progress. Consultants need to be efficient in their use of time, unintrusive, businesslike and practical. The effective consultant will stick as precisely as possible to the agreed contract.

Nor will the consultant hit people over the head with preconceived opinions. I have argued elsewhere for the importance of the hermaneutic model for consultants.[15] This means that they attend to what is there in the school, not shape the evidence to preconceived opinions. They are there as respondents: they must separate the 'teaching' and knowledge-giving role very precisely from the information-gathering and analytical role.

The closer the consultant comes to the thorny business of supporting the management of people, counselling and picking up (or working with) group dynamics, the more important the quality of these skills of 'detachment'. This is a special kind of detachment however, requiring the 'picking up of messages' as well as the ability to select information which will help improve situations and not make them worse. The consultant who began (as one did) 'well I really think you've got to do something about your wall display' is behaving in the old tradition of the patriarchal inspector. There may be institutions sufficiently dreadful to need marshalling and berating, but this, by and large, is not the job of the consultant. As Obholzer puts it:

'Whereas in commercial life a dash of omnipotence might be seen as very useful, in our field an accusation of omnipotence is almost guaranteed to stop people in their tracks.'[16]

The consultant, however, is not an empty vessel. Assessment requires advanced skills of observation in 'reading' what is actually there in its full complexity.

Paradoxically, consultancy is not value-free just because the consultant tries to be balanced, detached and positive. He needs to work through with his client the points of focus — to explain what he's doing from the beginning, and outline the map he is working on. Various maps are available for complex consultancy, ranging from background knowledge of the working of organisations[17] to use of the constructs of family therapy[18] for working with groups, organisational development, or even behavioural[19] and psychodynamic[20] psychology. For the most part, however, deep familiarity with the workings of schools, together with real knowledge of the transmission and development of a subject area — as well as personal skills in handling people (as individuals, or in groups) provide a good working base. Observation skills used in action research, the insights of 'what's going on' in group behaviour, and knowledge about the effectiveness of different kinds of management process are important areas for consultants to study. At my own school the staff evolved their own 'map' for classroom observation, a set of criteria (following HMI's own procedures) for assessing each other's classroom practice, which other schools have also found useful.

But it would be wrong too to suppose that consultancy can operate through check-off lists or books of rules. It is most important that the consultant has an internalised sense of procedures unencumbered by excessive bureaucracy or theoretical baggage. Successful consultants tend to be undogmatic, showing openness to learning themselves from experiences. This calls for a particular kind of person, showing high professional maturity.

It's certainly true that at a very advanced level, acting as a close analyst of some aspect of the school calls for very great skill. So does counselling individuals in a way that requires diagnosis and sustained support. So does any kind of sustained work with groups of teachers.

And the final requirement — to communicate sensitively and usefully — also calls for considerable skills in writing and communication to different audiences.

Consultants then may come from anywhere, but require certain natural predispositions, including personal warmth and the ability to listen — especially if they're to take on the more difficult counselling tasks. At advanced levels they would gain from training and supervision, and there is a need for the development of specialised training and support programmes for consultants and advisers in the educational field.

The final question for all consultancy, of course, is whether at the end of the day it makes any difference to quality of learning, to what happens in classrooms, to the school as a whole. If the consultancy is well planned and delivered, there is ample evidence that it can be crucial to the development of change, injecting new life and creative energy, bringing new accuracy of information and new quality of insight. This achieved, at the end of the day the successful consultant needs the ability to remove quietly from the scene, in the knowledge that the insight given has allowed the learners to take the learning on for themselves.

References

1   Dare, C .(1982)Techniques of consultation', *Association for Child Psychology and Psychiatry News,* 11 (Summer).
2   Winkley, D.R.(1985) *Diplomats and Detectives,* Robert Royce: Cassell, pp.90–93.
3   Obholzer, A.(1987) 'Institutional dynamics and resistance to change', *Psychoanalytical Psychotherapy,* 2(3).
4   McLean, A. et al. (1982) *Organisational Development in Transition: Evidence of an Evolving Profession,* Wiley 1982.
5   Everard, K.B. (1988) 'Training and Consultancy' in *Management Consultancy in Schools,* ed. Gray, H.L., Cassell, p.82.
6   Morris, G.(1988) 'Applying Business Consultancy to Schools', in Gray, H.L. op.cit., pp.93-104.
7   Everard, K.B.(1986) *Developing Management in Schools,* Blackwell.
8   cf, for example, Nias, J. et al. 'Primary School Staff Relationships', Research Project funded by the Economic and Social Research Council 1985-87.
9   cf *Special Children* (1988) 25(Nov.) p.22.
10 Winkley, Dr. L.M.(1989), Consultant Psychiatrist, Selly Oak Hospital, Birmingham: Report.
11 Salzberger-Wittenberg, I., et al. (1983) *The Emotional Experience of Learning and Teaching,* Routledge and Kegan Paul.
12 Dare, C., op. cit. p.6.
13 Winkley, D.R., op. cit. pp.25–36
14 Pike, Dr. L.A.(1988) 'How do we evaluate our work?' *Practical Issues in Primary Education,* Health Issues I, National Primary Centre Publications.
15 Winkley, D.R., op. cit. pp.95–98.
16 Obholzer, A., op. cit. p.20.
17 Dare, C., op. cit.
18 Mugatroyd, S. 'Consulting as Counselling' in Gray, H.L. op. cit.
19 Morris, op. cit.
20 Obholzer, op. cit.

6 Identifying needs in the context of appraisal

Eric Dodd

Eric Dodd's secondment to Newcastle's teacher appraisal pilot scheme has given him experience in the ways that the needs of both individuals and schools can be identified. He argues that appraisal can pinpoint ways in which teachers can make more effective contributions to the curriculum of their schools and that staff appraisal is an essential component in the process of school review.

The need for appraisal

In the past, experiences of change or developments have, in the main, been wholly dependent upon combinations of either individual initiatives, goodwill, or the essential informal co-operation of teachers within schools. As a result, a great reservoir of energy, knowledge and skills lay, in many cases, virtually untapped. Schools Council were instrumental in giving guidance as to how such energies, knowledge and skills could be harnessed for the benefit of schools in general, yet there are few formal systems in existence which attempt to establish support procedures and allow the collective capacity of teachers to be used to bring about change and development within schools.

If schools are to effectively utilise their total potential, they need to have in place a mechanism which has been shown to be capable of developing the corporate energy of all their teachers. Such a mechanism will however need to produce a freer flow of information, identify and diagnose strengths and needs and allow for constructive responses. It will naturally follow that such a mechanism will also need to be seen to promote improved learning and teaching through a more effective teaching force.

Although not to be regarded as a panacea for successful development and change, the introduction of a national system of appraisal for teachers and headteachers should provide a mechanism which assists in identifying and providing for the professional development needs of all schools and teachers. It will also be important however that any system of appraisal is not carried out merely for its own sake but rather that it 'is seen as a tool integral to the management of other initiatives and strategies'.[1] Achieving this will therefore depend to a great extent on how successful a school can be organising and developing its overall teaching force. This relationship is shown in Figure 1.

As schools are increasingly expected to produce enhanced provision for their pupils, such achievements can only result if perceptible changes occur in attitude, philosophy and management by everyone involved. Schools will need to develop, but it must also be recognised that this will only occur if teachers within schools develop, for as staff development occurs then a perceptible school development should also occur, the two being interdependent. Such developments will however only succeed if there is careful planning of an appraisal system, in addition to a recognition of the mechanism's overall requirements.

Figure 1: Creating an effective teaching force

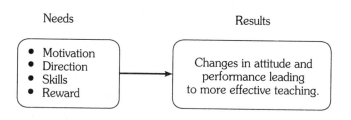

Needs | Results

- Motivation
- Direction
- Skills
- Reward

Changes in attitude and performance leading to more effective teaching.

Praise or blame?

There are two basic styles of approach to appraisal, one taking a 'deficit', the other a 'credit' stance. Each one has his own distinctive characteristics, as illustrated in Figure 2.

Figure 2: Deficit or credit approach

- A management method
  (Assessment: inspection, grades, pass/fail, discipline)
  (The teacher's M. O. T.)

- A method to aid management
  (Appraisal: individual valued, professional development, support, self-appraisal and potential)

A deficit approach is one that assumes that teachers are not very effective and lack total commitment. It is centred on searching for weaknesses, looking to identify weak teachers and producing evidence to remove them from the system. Characteristically it is carried out on a strict hierarchical basis and is, in effect, something that is 'done to teachers'. It also has strong links with reward systems and payment by results. Such an approach is not an unusual interpretation of what appraisal should be and is certainly an option which the Secretary of State appears to make available not only to LEAs but, within the present climate of LMS, perhaps more importantly to school governing bodies. From my own experience in the Pilot Project, I would warn against adopting this approach as it is an option which will result in tokenism by the majority of teachers and give rise to a failed system. After all, when necessary, most of us can 'go through the motions' if we are expected to meet a minimal 'pass' level. Indeed, if this overall approach were to be adopted, I cannot imagine there being many 'winners', least of all the pupils in our schools.

The alternative however is that of the 'credit' approach having professionalism inherent and commitment to the system openly acknowledged by those participating. It values each individual teacher's performance, qualities and potential and serves as a means of providing positive motivation. There is, in effect, a type of 'partnership' between those involved which produces meaningful professional development. This approach provides each teacher with support and feedback through recognising effective teaching and practice resulting in a perceptible enrichment of provision for all pupils. In addition, it allows for greater self, school and LEA awareness about individual performance and potential, allowing for better identified INSET needs, a more appropriate matching of these to INSET provision and providing guidance for career planning. Through such an approach there is the opportunity for a more open, honest reflection and review of performance, providing teachers with a firm base for improvement and encompassing a 'celebration of success'.

During my time of involvement with the National Appraisal Pilot Project in Newcastle upon Tyne LEA, it became obvious that a 'credit' approach did produce positive benefits for schools, teachers and pupils. These included:

- the professional development of teachers and headteachers
- the opportunities and means to explore institutional development and change
- improvement in classroom practice.

In addition, it has also been possible to identify some of the benefits that such a process has produced for pilot schools, including:

- improvement in pupils' learning experience
- identification of teaching skills and expertise
- identification of skills that need developing and the setting of realistic targets to assist this development
- recognition and support of effective practice
- clarification of school aims and objectives for all teachers
- identification of school priorities
- identification and co-ordination of resource needs
- identification and co-ordination of INSET needs
- clarification of teachers' and headteachers' jobs, roles and responsibilities
- provision of strategies to manage and cope with change.

Overall, appraisal outcomes have also helped to influence and structure INSET projections, books and stationery allowance spending and school development plans. In-school records on teachers have also been more up-to-date and accurate. Yet, to claim that the benefits, both by individuals and pilot schools, were achieved painlessly would be untrue. Even with the most willing of volunteers it has required changes, particularly in attitudes. It has, however, resulted in the adoption of a more open and perhaps more honest approach by all those involved. Certainly without the total commitment of each headteacher in each pilot school, the project in Newcastle would not have had the overall impact it has throughout the LEA.

Reviewing the whole school

Initial planning before introducing an appraisal system into a school requires not only careful but thorough attention to detail. Plans for any staff development programme needs to point to and reflect all aspects of a school's practice and performance. These can best be formed as a consequence of some form of initial whole school review which actually identifies both a school's strengths as well as those areas that require revision. Although not intended as prescriptive, Figure 3 attempts to highlight some of the probable areas that any form of whole school review should address.

Figure 3:   Areas for whole school review

   i   *School aims in the light of national and local initiatives.*

   ii   *Curriculum provision for all core and foundation subjects in addition to non-statutory subjects.*

   iii   *Job descriptions/specifications for all teachers within the school, including the headteacher.*

   iv   *Methods and means of communication, both external and internal.*

   v   *Financial organisation and management of funds and resources available to the school.*

   vi.   *External and internal parameters and constraints on the effective use of the overall school facilities and resources.*

It is important therefore that whole school reviews call upon relevant information and evidence and so allow an understanding of a school's total performance. Information must therefore include aspects and factors which are beyond a school's control, for it can only be through the overall review of a school that a full and meaningful collection of data will be created and be of value to all staff within the institution.

Outcomes from school reviews

Overall reviews should lead directly to a variety of developments once the strength and needs of the school have been identified. Such developments will, however, often occur at three main levels: corporate development, curriculum group/team development and the personal and professional development of each individual teacher. Some of the possible developments related to these three groups are illustrated in Figure 4 and indicate that these developments will often produce an 'overlap'.

There can and will be tensions however between not only the requirements but also the expectations of the three 'beneficiaries' and these will create dilemmas for those responsible for meeting each requirement or expectation. Corporate development will undoubtedly be a central purpose for any school, yet it will be important that whenever possible, governors, heads and teachers are in agreement and have a common understanding and balance of values and attitudes when identifying the possible developmental needs of the three 'beneficiaries'.

Figure 4: Outcomes from the review

'Beneficiaries'	Possible development
Corporate	• School aims • Overall curriculum provision • More appropriate INSET provision • More appropriate use of funds, finance and resources
Group/team	• More appropriate curriculum provision • Matching team skills to subject needs • Improved communication/support between team individuals
Individual	• Review of job descriptions • More appropriate use of skills and interests • Teaching skills and style • Overall potential, including career • More appropriate INSET

To achieve such a common understanding will not necessarily be an easy task, yet the creation of a 'climate of openness' should be regarded as an essential pre-requisite to any successful school change or development. It should also embrace an element of trust.

Methods of review

It should not be forgotten that it is the intricate web of interdependence and interaction, between different groups and individuals, which allows a school to function. In the same way, appraisal should not exist in isolation and its long-term impact will largely depend upon how far a school and its LEA can integrate an appraisal system, including its associated skills, with other forms of review, change and developments. This particular point was stressed by Cambridge Institute of Education in their *Evaluation of the Schoolteacher Appraisal Pilot Study* in 1989 when they stated:

'Teacher appraisal, headteacher appraisal, whole school review, school development plans, curriculum planning and

INSET planning are all related and might beneficially be linked in a coherent and co-ordinated strategy in order to achieve maximum impact.[2]

Such a co-ordinated and coherent strategy may be represented diagrammatically as shown in Figure 5. It will however require a form of review which addresses the 'present state of play' within a school.

Figure 5: A coherent strategy

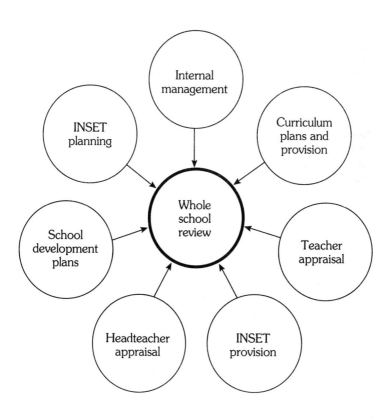

Approaches to reviews can vary enormously, in both content and emphasis, and appropriate methods need to be explored by schools before undertaking the exercise. For some schools it will be the overall review which provides the focus for team, group and individual appraisals. For others, however, an alternative strategy for review could be adopted. Whichever form is chosen will become an important issue, impacting upon the overall appraisal system. Positively promoting the use of a whole school review can form the contextual background against which appraisal can be introduced into a school and against which individual appraisals can take place. However, it can equally be beneficial for a school to begin by 'reviewing' individuals or groups of teachers, and from this information formulate a base for a 'whole school direction'. A whole school review may not therefore be felt appropriate prior to conducting appraisal — a form of review could conceivably result from individual appraisals. This possible 'alternative' approach is outlined in Figure 6.

Figure 6:   An alternative approach

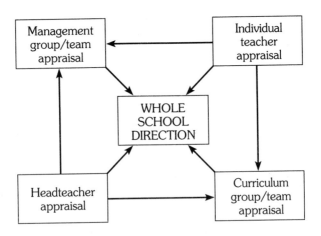

There are, nevertheless, a variety of documents designed to assist the process of whole school review, for example GRIDS.[3] This offers a process framework by which issues in a school may be clarified as well as investigated. The aim of such evaluation is to utilise a school review for developmental purposes. However, one of the practical difficulties with this and other review processes is that they can be extremely time consuming exercises and provide a poor yield of worthwhile information. Evidence from my own experience suggests that GRIDS tends to be more suitable for use in primary rather than in secondary schools. Perhaps it is because such documents tend to emphasise the collegiate approach to a school's operation which characterises the organisation in most primary schools.

Whatever structure of organisation and recording a school may adopt in undertaking whole school review, the needs of the school and the context in which it works need to be accurately reflected. In some schools a form of in-depth review, initiated and guided by the LEA, will already be in operation and these should become part of any new appraisal system.

Whatever system is adopted, undoubtedly whole school review should be, or become, a regular process. Continuous review is however of more relevance to teachers and headteachers since it develops from individuals themselves. It not only allows schools to take on board the on-going changes and demands of education more easily but also allows the integration and identification of both individual and school needs to occur at the same time. In this way the co-ordination of school and individual needs is more relevant and provides data for meaningful INSET while allowing the school's overall resources to be more effectively used.

Ownership

National Regulations and Guidelines for teacher and headteacher appraisal from the DES will provide LEAs with a framework for the formal appraisal of all teachers. However, any framework is open to interpretation. Such a situation should therefore provide us with opportunities to determine our own contextual solutions. Undoubtedly several differing 'sources' will provide interpretations of any regulation or guideline, yet the actual implementation of a system will be left to schools. Any opportunity afforded schools to modify systems in order to reflect the particular needs and management style of the institution should be regarded as a positive benefit. Left with a degree of flexibility, in both the organisation and management of the system, it provides astute practitioners opportunities for ownership and thereby allows the system to work both productively and constructively for the overall benefit of schools, teachers and pupils.

Ownership of an appraisal system is dependent however upon a particular climate within both an LEA and individual schools. It is important that a climate is created which allows the introduction of an appraisal system where everyone sees it as being for the ultimate benefit of all. It will indeed often only be within such a climate that practical solutions to problems will be found and in so doing ensure that an effective appraisal system flourishes. Consider, for example, a simple but practical problem as to where one might hold an appraisal discussion within a school. Does the school have a room which is relatively comfortable, readily accessible and totally free from interruptions in which a discussion could take place? If it does not, how might the school overcome such a problem? Some possible and creative solutions to this problem were proposed and tried during the Newcastle Pilot Project. These included the proposal for an 'appraisal caravan' (a bit like a visit from the school dentist) although this was never trialled. Use was however made of specific rooms allocated by the LEA at an education development centre, local community centre premises, shared facilities with other schools and some appraisal discussions taking place in teachers' homes.

Practical solutions need to be found, explored and used so that they compliment an appraisal process. Sometimes, proposed or expected solutions presented by an LEA turn out to be totally impractical when attempts are made to put them into practice. Therefore, those who are to be most affected by the appraisal system should be given some flexibility in their application, having the opportunity for themselves to find meaningful solutions within the context in which they work.

Starting up

The appraisal system in Newcastle was deliberately co-ordinated in a way which did permit ownership and commitment to occur by allowing schools to develop the LEA's basic framework in the context in which each was working. The LEA's guidelines were therefore able to be 'moulded' in order to meet specific conditions found within each individual institution. Great efforts were also made to keep written guidelines both clear and concise and teacher comments and suggestions were encouraged.

Ownership and commitment to the system's operation therefore depended upon those directly involved being given the opportunity to make their own personal contribution to the format and structure of the system. Clarity of purpose is initially a crucial issue and teachers will be preoccupied with this during the introduction of an appraisal system, whether within individual schools or throughout an LEA. Alongside general aims there must, therefore, be specific objectives to give the system structure. However, although schools need to have some freedom in maintaining systems of appraisal, limits must be set which maintain a national system. Monitoring and reviewing any appraisal system is therefore important at both school and LEA level. By so doing, any suggestions for improvements can therefore be shared and implemented. For example, in Newcastle, by initiating an appraisal working group within each pilot school, the professional responsibility for individual and school developments of the LEA's formative appraisal framework was given to teachers and headteachers within those pilot schools. Through careful co-ordination and monitoring of pilot schools' progress, shared experiences and recommendations for improvements to the system were achieved. There was, in addition, the natural and obvious need, indeed the requirement, for the LEA to ensure that the overall system was not only co-ordinated and monitored, but also fully evaluated through the correct and appropriate LEA management and consultative groups. This overall approach provided the LEA with an added bonus in that they too were provided with clearer and more up-to-date information on the talents and skills of the teaching force — something they had never had before.

Certainly the 'credit' approach adopted by Newcastle placed the individual teacher and headteacher firmly at the centre of the appraisal system's design and operation. It undoubtedly paid dividends for those individuals involved in the pilot schools. It was, nevertheless, not surprising to discover, both during training and in the initial operation of the system, that teachers and headteachers were preoccupied not with development, but rather with those things that were not going so well and, or, in which they were not being as successful as they, or others, thought they perhaps ought to be. It was therefore an important initial task to begin to get teachers and headteachers to identify the many things that were going well and in which they were being successful. A balance needed to be achieved between success, needs and direction for each individual. It also meant quite a cultural shock, for many now had permission to celebrate success, develop their self-confidence and self-esteem and actually to enjoy the process. Individuals, for the first time in their professional career, began to appreciate the potential of the overall appraisal system, both for themselves and their school. They were motivated, or even rejuvenated in some instances, into a more positive and effective way of fulfilling their roles within their schools.

A major factor in identifying the balance of successes, needs and direction within these roles was the development of a job description (or specification) for each individual. These naturally involved time and some negotiation occurring in the early stages of both the appraisal training and the system's operation. They are, however, essential for they provide the individual framework to which appraisal can be directly related and enable meaningful findings and outcomes to occur.

Teacher appraisal in action

Figure 7 outlines the process adopted in the Newcastle Pilot Project for teacher and headteacher appraisal and has direct relevance to Figure 8.

Interwoven within the operation of the process are several issues to the successful completion and outcomes for each individual and each school. The initial responsibility of LEAs, in part through their headteachers, should be to attempt to allay the fears and concerns teachers will have towards any appraisal system. For many teachers any appraisal system will be viewed as threatening and possibly judgemental in the extreme. The distinct possibility that teachers are going to be judged, not so much by themselves, but rather by 'others' having their own subjectivity, prejudices and biases, is a real threat! A system must be seen to carry with it the objectivity and criteria by which we, as professional individuals, can and should be appraised. Job descriptions and specifications can go a long way to reduce initial fears. Yet, perhaps far too often DES, HMI, LEAs, governing bodies and even ourselves seem to indicate that there are beings who can be identified as 'good teachers', without necessarily giving meaningful criteria by which we and others may tell. Perhaps it would make life so much easier, but boring, if every teacher was virtually the same. We ought not to attempt to clone our teaching force and yet we do need to address the question, 'What is, or makes, a good teacher?' We do need some criteria on which to base the appraisal of a teacher's performance and yet such criteria should not preclude or stifle individual approaches to a job or indeed possible eccentricities in methodology. There is a real danger that we could well be presented with a simplistic checklist of skills, styles and attitudes with which we will measure and be measured!

Figure 7: Appraisal in Newscastle (1987–1989)

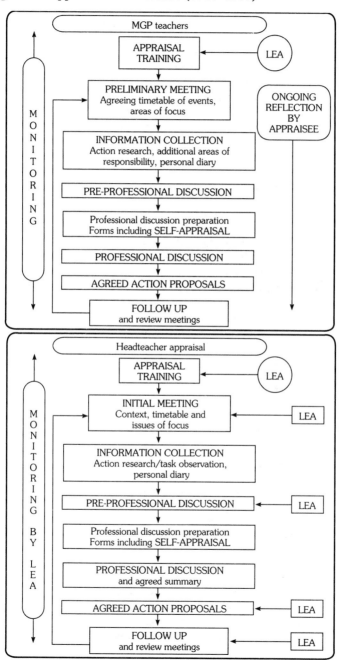

Figure 8: Times within the appraisal process

It should be noted that the times shown are in HOURS and relate to ONE FULL APPRAISAL

EE—Appraisee   ER—Appraiser

	TEACHER		HEADTEACHER		
	EE	ER	EE	ER	LEA
1. Initial review meeting	1	1	3	3	2
2. Classroom observation (All additional time on top of TWO OBSERVATIONS)	2	5	2	5	–
3. Task Observation (All additional time on top of TWO observations of 1 hour)	–	–	2	5	–
4. Collection of other information	1	1	2	8	–
5. Pre-Appraisal Discussion meeting	½	½	1	1	1
6. Self-Appraisal	1	–	2	–	–
7. Appraisal discussion	2½	2½	3	3	–
8. Agreeing and producing appraisal record	½	1½	2	5	–
9. Producing agreed action proposals	–	–	1	3	1
10. Follow-up review	1½	1½	3	3	3
11. Monitoring	–	–	1	2	2
INDIVIDUAL TOTALS	10	13	22	38	9
TOTAL FOR PROCESS	23 hours		69 hours		

Time

One of the major requirements of any appraisal system will be the need for appropriate and adequate time in order to carry out the process. Organising and managing the necessary time to complete all the appraisal process components, for every teacher within a school, will demand high qualities of organisational and managerial skills. An example of the amounts of time needed to complete each appraisal process during the Newcastle Pilot Project is shown in Figure 8. The times have been averaged out and when necessary rounded up for simplification.

With such a commitment it may well be worth considering that a school, when beginning the appraisal process, be given the opportunity of a 'trial period' during which individuals can become familiar with the process and explore, in practice, the other requirements that will be involved; for example approaches to observations. Therefore, determining the priorities and needs of a system's components, operation and implications, while matching them to the context in which a school operates is important. Any attempt to short-cut the process, or under-cut the resourcing will be damaging.

Classroom/task observation

The majority of teachers and indeed many headteachers have a teaching commitment. In addition some teachers and headteachers will also have specific managerial tasks to perform. Observations of teachers and headteachers carrying out these roles and associated responsibilities will need to form part of the overall collection of information regarding an individual's performance. It is important to determine what types of observations can be undertaken as they need to reflect a fair and equitable representation of an individual's role. For many individuals the major ity of observations will be those primarily associated with classroom practice. Nevertheless, there will be a smaller number, mostly headteachers, who may have observations which are entirely concerned with management performance.

Whatever observations are undertaken, it will be essential that they are directly related to agreed and known areas of focus. Job descriptions can therefore be crucial in aiding and identifying areas of focus. These areas are important as any observation needs to provide adequate and appropriate data to assist the appraisee's self-appraisal, positively contribute to the appraisal discussion and assist professional development.

A process for carrying out both types of observations is illustrated in Figure 9, referred to as an 'action research' model.

Figure 9: Observations (An action research approach)

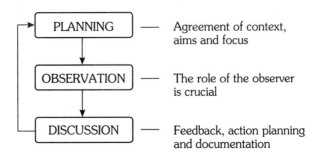

This model was adopted for all types of observations during the Newcastle Pilot Project and proved to be not only non-threatening but positively promoted the observation sessions. It provided meaningful data and feedback for the observed individual and assisted both the overall appraisal process and the appraisal discussion.

Before the observation it was important however that both appraisee and appraiser worked together in order to compile a research approach for issues under consideration. Aspects of the situation about which data was to be gathered, the form and the occasion of the observation were also agreed. The appraisee and appraiser therefore concentrated on particular and precise issues, identifying and defining the criteria to be used, prior to any observation. Whenever appropriate, such issues were seen as part of a continuing, developmental cycle.

The identification of issues and the criteria to be used are very important for, as has already been highlighted, there is the danger that performance criteria will be pre-determined and presented as a checklist against which we will all be measured.

In the action research approach the fundamental role of the observer is to collect unbiased data about the observed teacher or headteacher. After the observation both appraisee and appraiser work together to provide each other with feedback on the situation observed. This is achieved by checking out and discussing both sets of perceptions of what took place.

In order that maximum benefit is gained from the observation, it will however be essential that as part of the follow up action, the relevant observation record is completed. This record was completed, in Newcastle, by the appraiser and included a plan for development based on the post-observation discussions. The records were discussed, agreed and signed by both the appraisee and appraiser following every post-observation discussion.

It is important that all records of observations are referred to by the appraisee when preparing for the appraisal discussion. Indeed, they may wish to bring these records and introduce them into the appraisal discussion. The appraiser however will also need to refer to these records when preparing for the appraisal discussion, as it will be expected that some of the objectives agreed during the appraisal discussion will be based on the development and improvement plans arising from all observations.

Self-appraisal

Self-appraisal by the individual has always been central to the appraisal process adopted by Newcastle and its relevance and importance to the overall process of formal appraisal was regarded as crucial. It must take place before the appraisal discussion; however it is never easy for teachers to reflect positively, constructively and in-depth about their performance. It is therefore important that the emphasis on this part of the appraisal process and the skills involved be given appropriate time during initial training.

It has not been surprising to find, from the experience of teachers in Newcastle, that when individual self-appraisal has been conducted thoroughly, it has, on occasions, been the most important part of the whole appraisal. It is something new for teachers and headteachers to reflect in depth on their performance and it is not an easy task to accomplish in a relatively short period of time. Yet it has the potential to be a major factor in determining and enhancing the overall quality of the appraisal discussion.

It can be difficult to conduct self-appraisal in the hurly-burly of school hours. Certainly any time given in the school to carry out self-appraisal only allows the identification of areas for further reflection. Most of the self-appraisal needs to be made away from school for it is only then that one can reflect in depth on some of the more thought-provoking questions about oneself. These need not however be too overpowering, nor prescriptive. They can in fact be very 'simple' as Figure 10 shows.

Figure 10:   Key questions for self-appraisal

1.   What are the key tasks and responsibilities of my job?

2.   Can I describe these key tasks and responsibilities?

3.   What things have gone well?

4.   What has not gone well?

5.   How can I do my job better?

6.   What can help me to do my job better?

7.   How can I help myself become more effective?

8.   Who can help me be more effective?

9.   What should be my key aims for next year?

10.   How would I like to see my career developing?

11.   Have I any skills or expertise which are not being fully utilised?

12.   What management decisions need to be made to provide me better facilities and/or equipment to improve my effectiveness?

13.   Does my job description need updating and why?

14.   What obstacles prevented me from accomplishing my aims this past year?

15.   What would I like to be doing in two or three years time?

It is also useful to discuss seriously some aspects of the above self-appraisal questions with colleagues. By doing so it not only provides preparation for the appraisal discussion by gaining the external perspectives of others on one's performance, but also provides further opportunities for greater in-depth reflection The process of self-appraisal can be emotionally taxing and it can be difficult at times to draw back from self-analysis overload. This can be especially true during the first round of the appraisal process. Nevertheless, although exhausting, the experience can be extremely beneficial. It allows the creation of meaningful and rational 'triggers' making clearer the aims and objectives within one's role and possible targets and developmental needs for the discussion. It is also possible to enter the appraisal discussion with a clearer picture of what the teacher wants to achieve during and by the end of the discussion, while in no way pre-empting the possible issues of discussion the appraiser might wish to raise.

My self-appraisal complimented the areas of focus agreed between my appraiser and myself prior to the appraisal discussion and I felt secure in this agreed and negotiated framework. This latter point is again important for it was through this supportive element, involving negotiation, that I was afforded meaningful opportunities to identify my own professional development needs. It also provided a means by which relevant aspects of my performance and needs could be recorded, records which were not based on hearsay or innuendoes, but on objective data and evidence collected through agreed criteria and sources negotiated early on in my appraisal round.

The appraisal record

Meaningful records of appraisal discussions are crucial and the form that the recording takes may vary while still meeting the needs of each school and each individual. A common format across an LEA will be essential, yet it should provide for contextual aspects of individuals or schools to be given, if appropriate.

The final record of the appraisal discussion should be an agreed summary of all the main points addressed during that discussion and the conclusions reached. In addition, an appraised individual should take the opportunity to play a part in producing the final record as well as indicating that they are content with the record. The form that the appraisal record might take is illustrated in Figure 11.

The appraisal record, which will be held 'on file', should include additional material if the appraised teacher so wishes; for example, their own self-appraisal document. The recording of self-appraisal findings is, however, a very personal issue and although one would expect to be honest with oneself during 'reflection', how and whether one should include these within the final appraisal record is a pertinent question. How open and honest can, or should, one be? How confidential will, or should all documents and data be? It is therefore very important that one is fully aware not only what the purposes of the overall appraisal system are but also who will be permitted access to appraisal documents and in what circumstances. If the appraisal is to be used exclusively for review and development then 'open' access is unlikely to be an issue. If appraisal is to be linked with possible promotion or dismissal then obviously those that are appraised would want clear control over access.

Figure 11:　An example of an appraisal record

APPRAISAL DISCUSSION SUMMARY SHEET

School: _____

Date of discussion _____ 19

1. Summary of main points of the discussion

2. Objectives (both short and long term)

3. Agreed action proposals

4. The appraisee may record any comments he/she wishes in the space below

5. Signed: _____　　　　_____
　　　　　Appraisee　　Date　　　　Appraiser　　Date

Any records of the appraisal discussion will need to conform to the requirements of both LEA and school. The inclusion of additional data should therefore be left to the discussion of the appraised individual. A carefully formulated and binding 'code of practice' regarding both records and access to records will be a necessity. The legality and right of the LEA to have access to any pertinent documents written by, or on behalf of individual employees has already been determined; however, it is important that an appraised teacher has 'ownership' of these records. A code of practice should ensure that confidentiality of records is achieved. In part, this can be achieved by having all records stored in a secure location in the teacher's own school. To enhance further the acceptance of the confidentiality of such records, it is essential that only an agreed group of individuals should be permitted access to such records but that this should only occur after prior consultation with the appraised individuals.

Confidentiality and access to appraisal records and documents needs to be dealt with sensitively and professionally and the role that a headteacher will play in achieving this is vital. It is possible that school governing bodies will make requests for appraisal records to be made available to them. Any code of practice must make specific reference to the sorts of information from appraisal records governing bodies should receive.

Outcomes from appraisal

Within an appraisal record will be agreed targets and suggestions for professional development in addition to the probable, or necessary, resources needed to meet these requirements. All of these will need to be conveyed, in appropriate ways, to the respective individual, or bodies of individuals, responsible for meeting these either within a school or the LEA. The most appropriate way of achieving this, from Newcastle's experience, is for these requirements to be recorded on separate forms.

From experience, initial expectations by the majority of teachers is that where areas of professional development are identified they will be directed to some form of INSET course. For some this will undoubtedly be the case; however, alternative professional development activities may be indicated. Some examples of these from Newcastle's experience include:

- visits between different teachers in different classes or year groups within a school to learn from differing teaching styles and techniques;
- visits between teachers and their feeder schools to both observe and participate in the teaching of pupils within particular subjects and so gain a fuller understanding of curricular aspects, provision, teaching styles and approaches;
- teachers becoming actively involved in the provision of in-service training both within their own and other schools, utilising their skills, understanding and interest in particular curricular or administrative issues;
- changes in role or experiences within a school to assist in career appreciation and development.

If meaningful outcomes to appraisal are to occur, the appraised teacher, along with others, must work together to ensure that energetic follow-up to appraisal occurs. It may perhaps often rest with the efforts of the appraised individual as to whether outcomes, or targets, are met. There will therefore be a need to build into the overall appraisal timetable and process a number of review meetings. These meetings will be important as numerous factors can affect target achievement, particularly changes occurring within a school. By providing review meetings, targets can be reassessed and realigned, taking into account and considering the relevant factors that affect them.

I have heard some teachers react strongly against the suggestion that they themselves should take some major responsibility in achieving outcomes or targets resulting from appraisal. They have claimed that this will merely be INSET on the cheap. Such a view should be tempered with the knowledge that resources to enable meaningful development, both within the LEA and the school, from our experience, has allowed more appropriate use of resources and funding being made available to schools and individual teachers within those schools.

Managing the system

The ultimate test of any appraisal system will be whether it actually produces benefits and professional development opportunities for both individual teachers and their schools. In turn it should also result in perceptible increases in the effectiveness of a school and its provision for its pupils. The implementation of an appraisal system produces high expectations of change. Unless extra resources are provided to meet at least some of these expectations then frustration and perhaps disillusionment will result. LEAs will have a responsibility to ensure that resources exist and are available in order to allow a system to function fully and properly. Schools however must also ensure that they use these available resources creatively!

A summary of the effects of appraisal

Our experience, gained during the National Appraisal Pilot Project, allows the following lessons to be stated about a 'credit' approach to appraisal:

1. Both the underlying philosophy and purpose are valid.
2. A sense of ownership and commitment to the process is important.
3. Teachers and headteachers are extremely apprehensive prior to their involvement in the process. Gaining direct experi-

ence of the process does however reassure them.
4. The process alone can be productive.
5. A short cycle is easier to manage and will initially be more productive than an extended one.
6. A fairly long period of climate-setting may be required in order to reduce anxieties.
7. Adequate preparation for all those involved in the process is vital.
8. Appraisees need appropriate training in addition to appraisers.
9. The first cycle of appraisal should be regarded as a 'trial' period.
10. Observations can be extremely creative experiences and can have several wider applications than simply to that of appraisal.
11. A real system of support can be created through participating in the process.
12. Time requirements can be considerable.
13. Appraisal should be an in-house activity.
14. The process requires careful organisation and management.
15. The understanding of what INSET is and can be may be enhanced.
16. The provision of INSET can be greatly improved.
17. Appraisal should be absorbed into the culture and developments of a school.
18. Appraisal should not be regarded as a 'bolt-on' extra.

References

1   *Schoolteacher Appraisal : A National Framework (1989)*, HMSO.
2   Cambridge Institute of Education (1989) *Evaluation of the Schoolteacher Appraisal Pilot Study*
3   McMahon, A. (1988) *Guidelines for Review and Internal Development in Schools: Primary Schools Handbook,* (GRIDS) Longman.

Further bibliography

Developments in the Appraisal of Teachers — an HMI Report (1989), HMSO.
Hall, J. (1989) *LEAP — Management in Education INSET Initiaties.*
Staff Manual — Teachers and Headteachers, (1989) Newcastle-upon-Tyne LEA.

7 Developing a partnership with parents

Mike Sullivan

Working in partnership with parents to improve pupil performance just seems the most natural way for primary schools to operate. The first part of this chapter identifies those areas which are concerned with explanation and justification to parents of the way in which a school works. Later, ways and means of involving parents more actively in children's learning are described.

It is a hard fact of life that the survival and prosperity of individual schools is becoming increasingly dependent on the support and goodwill of parents. Zoning, catchment areas and other means of artificially protecting pupil rolls have virtually been swept away. Except for the remotest of rural schools parents use their feet or any other means of transport available to take their children to the school which appears to offer the greatest benefits. The vast majority of schools rely on nothing less than their popularity in the community for their existence.

It is against this background that schools must not only develop and extend the curriculum that they offer but also win the approval and support of the community that they serve.

Maintaining and extending parental support need not be some white-knuckle ride with schools scampering helter skelter to snatch an advantage over rivals through the adoption of over-aggressive marketing styles, but more of a planned systematic approach of sharing and informing.

School policy

There can be few primary schools that don't pay at least lip-service to the notion of parental involvement in the life of the school. There appear to be two different approaches, the first is where parents are viewed as consumers, with the school providing the parents with information about children's progress and the school's philosophy and practice. The second approach sees the parent as a resource; parents are encouraged to take a direct role in the children's education through their involvement in classrooms, involvement in children's learning and also by being actively engaged in the raising of funds. In both approaches power and initiative rests squarely with the professionals. Wolfendale (1985)[1] produced the chart in Figure 1 to illustrate the range of parental contact and involvement in schools.

The stances that schools adopt are often intuitive; many schools bumble along without any clearly articulated plan or strategy for parental involvement, ideas are taken up or abandoned without a long-term view being formed. The results are often disappointing and the raising of enthusiasms and energies on future occasions less easily achieved. Too often, demands are made on parents to support a curriculum and a system of organisation and management that they don't really understand.

Greater communication and greater understanding sometimes have drawbacks. Parents can have expectations about the ways in which schools work which are completely unfounded in reality. When communication between school and home is poor then parents can blithely assume that their pre-conceived notions about education are being carried out in practice. Efficient and effective communication quickly destroys these delusions and conflict may arise. The greater the involvement of parents in schools, the stronger their power-base in bringing an influence on decision-making in schools.

The trick is convincing parents that they want what you want — easy to say and, thankfully, in most cases fairly easy to accomplish.

If there is to be effective contact with parents then there needs to be an overall school policy. Aims and objectives should be formulated and discussions on these held between teachers, governors and parents. The first objective must be winning the hearts and minds in the staff room. Teachers are busy people and they need convincing that time invested in parents will produce great advantages in children's learning. A worthwhile policy will take into account a whole range of activities and levels of involvement.

Figure 1: Parental involvement in schools

nil contact	minimal contact	moderate contact	moderate involvement	considerable involvement	partnership
	open evenings, concerts, plays, written reports	- - - - - - - -> - - - - - - - ->	parent hears reading, helps with painting, cooking, newsletters - - - - - - - ->	home reading, maths, parents' room, home liaison teacher, parent workshops, - - - - -> community base	- - - - - - - -> - - - - ->

Talking to parents

Nothing can match conversation as a means of communication; there are many opportunities that arise where teachers and parents can talk about the progress of individual children and the learning experiences that are taking place both at school and at home. The very first day that parents register their child at school is an occasion for a visit to the classrooms, a chance to talk about what the child already knows and enjoys and a chance to talk about routines and the ways in which parents and the school can offer each other mutual support. Particularly important is a genuine invitation to parents to contribute to the child's assessment record through requests to provide pre-school drawings, photos and even tapes of children talking at home.

The parents will be gaining their first impressions of the school at this time. Attitudes will be formed as to whether the school is a friendly, welcoming place. Notices giving visitors clear directions to the head's and secretary's rooms put newcomers more at their ease. A junk-free entrance hall containing attractive displays of children's work and comfortable chairs and interesting booklets of children's work placed outside the headteacher's room give reassuring messages about the school as a caring and thoughtful organisation.

Once the child has started and settled in there are those casual and unplanned moments just before school starts and just after it finishes when teachers and parents can catch a few words with each other about small incidents and concerns. These are also the moments when conversations can also include small talk about families, pets and those everyday events that reveal that teachers too are human beings with lives that extend beyond the school walls. If schools have rigid policies that discourage parents from entering the buildings at these times then a golden opportunity for establishing and extending good relationships is lost. It is important that the Headteacher is around the school and approachable at these moments too, just to check that everything is going well.

Some starter items for staff discussion on maximising parental interest

How do parents discover what's going on in school?

> Does the school provide newsletters on a regular enough basis?
> Are newsletters written in a friendly and readable style?
> Do the newsletters look cheap and tatty?
> Do the newsletters communicate about curriculum or are they usually appeals for money and reminders of rules and regulations?
> Does the school have its own prospectus in addition to the LEA issue and if so is it attractive and up-to-date?
> How does the school deal with eyeball-to-eyeball contact with parents?
> Are parents encouraged to visit corridors and classrooms?
> Can the arrangements for parents' evenings be better organised?

Discussing children's progress

It is vital that parents and teacher have time to meet together to review progress and engage in some forward planning. In most schools it's traditional to hold parents' evenings. Teachers are able to give their full attention to parents in that they are free from their classes and parents will be free from their work.

Some schools have broken away from this pattern in the realisation that a large number of parents prefer to go to the school during the day, e.g. single mums (and dads) with babies/toddlers, women living in inner city areas without their own transport, Asian women etc.

Arranging progress reviews with parents during the school day does present schools with problems of providing staff cover. One way around this is to invite the parents of just one or two children in during the normal school day so that they can talk with the teacher and also observe their child at work.

Parents in many schools are often disappointed with the organisation of review meetings. Pressure of time results in teachers telling and parents listening; in a way it seems that parents are made accountable for their children rather than the teacher giving account of the intellectual and social development of the child. It is still rare to find these occasions used as a meeting where parents and teacher collaborate about ways and means of working jointly together to bring about improvements in the child's progress.

Any review of arrangements for parents' evenings or other regular meeting between parent and teacher could consider the following points :

1.   Timing — how frequently should meetings be held? Should there be a number of meetings spread over a week so that parents have more choice?

2.   How much time should be allocated for each appointment? Long queues of impatient parents do no one any good.

3.   Should the school offer parents an appointment time or should parents select a time from an appointment list displayed in the school some days earlier?

4.   Are parents given early enough notice of the date of a parents' evening? Is the initial letter welcoming and encouraging or more like a summons to a magistrate's court? Is there a follow-up-letter if there is no response to the first invitation?

5.   Should an effort be made to ensure that at least one piece of work from each child is attractively displayed and labelled in the classroom?

6.   Do teachers have a checklist so that they can ensure that all the important issues are covered?

7.   Do teachers have evidence at hand to support statements about improvements or setbacks in children's progress? Even though schools are obliged to report back in specific terms to parents under the arrangements for the National Curriculum, there is still a high chance that talk of attainment levels will, without care, provide parents with a very confused picture.

8.   Do teachers keep a record of the interview with parents, noting parents' concerns and interests and the ways in which parents have offered to support their child's learning? Are these notes entered into the child's file?

9.   Are parents offered a written report at the end of the meeting?

10. Is there any action to provide those parents that didn't attend the evening a further opportunity to meet a member of staff through dropping into school during the working day or through home visiting? Is there a staff post-mortem of the evening to identify concerns and possible improvements in its organisation?

Writing to parents

Impact is vital in getting the message home. The A4 sheet of bleatings complaining about parents parking in front of the school or appeals for yet more jumble just clutters up a vital channel of communication. Children's safety is of course of prime importance, but catching the irresponsible parkers on the spot and button-holing them then and there is more likely to produce results than grizzling on at all the parents through the newsletter. Fund-raising is important too, but items about money-raising and social events can more successfully hit the target if details are run-off and distributed as special 'flyers' produced with eye-catching illustrations and few words in bold print. Older children are more than capable of producing attractive 'flyers' using a computer and a word processor programme.

The newsletter, once stripped of a great deal of verbiage, can focus on ways and means of focusing attention on children's learning. Interesting activities can be highlighted, including details of class visits and projects to be undertaken and the ways that parents can help, invitations to parents to visit classrooms to see children's displays and interesting activities taking place.

Enlarging photocopies of newsletters and placing them on prominent display in the school windows will make sure that those parents whose children manage to lose letters between classroom and school door have a chance to know what's going on!

The essential information about school hours, contact addresses, phone numbers, rules and regulations are best kept to a brochure distributed annually and to new parents to the school. Sensitivity and care needs to be shown with all communications to ensure that the school meets the needs of those parents that are unable to read English. This minority group is not only made up of those whose mother tongue is not English, but also a proportion of traveller families, and those families that have some sort of handicap which interferes with reading.

If the school has the benefit of a home-school liaison teacher then the clear communication of information to minority groups should form an important part of this teacher's role.

Curriculum workshops for parents

Improving Primary Schools (ILEA 1985)[2] identified the following as common worries of parents: pace of learning, insufficient memorisation of arithmetic tables, the teaching of grammar and spelling and puzzlement about schools' approach to mathematics. Added to this, through the introduction of the National Curriculum, must be concerns about the teaching of science and technology.

There is a groundswell of opinion outside schools that not only are knowledge and skills of vital importance but that learning can best be achieved through toil and rigid discipline. Most of us working in schools believe that a curriculum which is planned, active and engaging and is also involved with forming positive attitudes through which skills and knowledge are gratuitously absorbed is the best way of teaching and learning.

Through workshops for parents the school can employ the techniques it advocates in assuring parents that it is on the right track.

Running a workshop

Purpose

The idea for a workshop can arise from discussion about the curriculum at a governors' meeting, interest by parents shown at a parents' evening, coffee morning or school function, or from the staff in wanting to share ideas about a new scheme or wanting to enlist parental help and enthusiasm.

Planning

A small group of staff and parents can undertake responsibility for the arrangements for the workshop including the provision of refreshments. It is essential that all members of staff clearly understand the purpose of the workshop and the role that they are expected to play.

Timing

The choice of date and time is crucial for success. If the target audience is narrow then it may be possible to organise a session following a 'Family Assembly'. The parents themselves are best at suggesting the most suitable time for a meeting, though even after the most careful planning there is no way of meeting everyone's needs.

Publicity

Parents' curiosity needs to be captured along with the promise that their time will be well spent. 'Do come to our parents' workshop and bring a teapot' is a good example of an intriguing invitation.

Displays

Examples of a wide range of children's work should be on display including photographs of children working at tasks associated with the workshop.

Presentation

A workshop shouldn't be an occasion for teachers to talk at parents. The presentation needs to be interesting and is best delivered in terms of 'your children' rather than 'the school'.

A video of the children at the school engaged in some of the activities that are being described is always a success.

An overhead projector is an invaluable tool for presenting information in a visual form, although one of the pitfalls is that you can end up talking to the screen rather than to the audience.

Activities

The activities are best when aimed at the parents' own interest and experience level. In science tasks such as building the best aeroplane from a sheet of paper, building the best elastic-powered model car or finding the best teapot will soon generate a great deal of group discussion and practical activity. Maths tasks such as finding the height of the school or the weight of a single sheet of paper will also generate involvement. Work on 'nonsense' text that reveals the rules of grammar and the ways in which adults read are useful starters in language workshops.

Equipment

It is essential that there is not only enough equipment for parents to use but that it actually works. Scissors that don't cut and wobbly compasses will reveal a great deal about school organisation, unless the whole point of the workshop is to show how inadequate funding has resulted in poor resourcing!

Closing the workshop

The purpose of the workshop should be restated and profuse thanks to all those involved given. The ways in which parents can help their children should be identified and parent interest in their children's learning and in the school encouraged.

Parents and power

Recent legislation has given parents the potential to exert a great deal of control over the curriculum and management of schools. There has been an increase in the proportion of governors that are directly elected as parents; in addition to those elected, other parents can be co-opted to the governing body.

The governors have responsibility for the curriculum, for the hiring of staff and, in most cases, for the finances of the school. In practice, there is hardly any evidence of power struggles taking place between governors and staff, in most cases governors are happy to delegate many of their responsibilities.

Good relationships between governors and staff depends on trust. This trust can be something akin to blind faith or trust based on open communications. Parent governors have day-to-day relationships with the school and, even if they are not regular visitors, have a constant stream of information directed at them from their children and their neighbours.

Gratuitously acquired information fails to make governors 'experts' and time needs to be spent in helping governors to identify important issues and provide relevant background so that rational, informed decisions can be made. Invitations to school events such as concerts and plays are little help in providing governors with the skills and knowledge needed to get to grips with, say, judging whether money would be better spent on more books for the school library or a new computer, or trying to balance the arguments used in support of 'real reading books' against the arguments used to support structured reading schemes.

All of us are put off by the sheer volume of paper that is directed at us and parent governors are no exception.

Every governor needs to be invited to see children and staff working and it's a good idea to ask governors to adopt a year group. The sense of partnership is increased and individual governors can develop an in-depth relationship with a particular group of children.

Governors' meetings can be quite intimidating events for parents. There is a need for a certain amount of formal structure to ensure the effective and efficient movement through the business of the meeting, but often the volume of written reports and legislation that are covered turns the event into a boring occasion unless time is spent in discussing real children and the ways in which they are learning. It's not the core that is particularly important but the seeds that lie there.

The room in which governors' meetings are held should be full of displays of children's work and photographs of school activities; the governors' attention should be directed to these.

One fairly new responsibility of governors is the obligation to report back formally to parents. Even when the reporting back is linked to other events, attendance can be quite low unless there is some matter of controversy to be dealt with at the meeting.

A checklist for parent-governor involvement

1. Are parent governors regularly invited to the school to learn at first hand?
2. Are parent governors encouraged to learn what others in the locality think about the school — and put them right if they are misinformed?
3. Are all governors encouraged to take an interest in the children through 'adopting' a specific age group or aspect of the curriculum for a set period and then reporting back informally at governors' meetings?
4. Do all governors receive copies of letters as a matter of routine?
5. Are parent governors encouraged to keep the head and staff aware of potential trouble brewing?
6. Are parent governors informed at an early stage about potential changes in the curriculum?
7. Are parent governors encouraged to mobilise public support on specific issues?
8. Are parent governors always clear about the implications of implementing policies that are likely to be controversial?
9. Are all parents aware of the purpose and functions of the governing body ? Are the addresses of governors displayed prominently around the school so that contact by other parents can be made easily?

Parents and home work

It's natural for parents to want their children to do well at school and for the parents to give help to their children with reading and basic arithmetic. It's at this stage that opportunities arise that will accelerate children's learning or, if mishandled, confusion, conflict and frustration will arise. Making the most of the opportunity depends, to a great extent, on the school carefully spelling out its teaching strategies, identifying ways in which parents can not only provide supplementary help but also ways in which parents can initiate worthwhile learning activities. Ruth Merttens in Chapter 8 gives excellent examples of the ways in which parents have been involved in the development of their children's understanding of maths.

If the school is unwilling or unable to give the lead in providing guidance as to how parents can help their children then parents will look elsewhere for assistance. Publishers are already bypassing the schools and a trip to a branch of any of the major chains of newsagents or even the supermarkets will yield well packaged and attractively produced books of activities and projects designed for parents to work through with their children. The contents of these books supplied to satisfy this ready market doesn't always follow best primary practice. In fact looking at some examples of these books would be a useful workshop session with parents.

Parents and reading

It is certainly common practice for children to take reading books home, but what is the parent actually expected to do? Are they to listen to children rehearse pages already read at school or to push on to virgin ground? What sorts of prompts and primes are the parents expected to employ to help their child with reading, what sort of errors should be corrected and how? In the worst situations sending reading books home provides little more than an opportunity for parents to check that the teacher is actually listening to their child read the book on a regular basis, just chalking up the number of pages read. All the incidental reading that occurs from the immersion in a rich language environment of school is disregarded. Both parent and child are driven on with relentless determination in the pursuit of the next reading level and this attitude is in part fostered by the unthinking school.

Much has been done to develop more effective ways of combining the efforts of parents and teachers in encouraging reading skills. There are three distinct approaches, and a whole range of variations on these themes.

Parent listening

In this approach the process of beginning to read is explained at parents' meetings first of all, together with the ways in which parents can help their children to master these techniques. The importance of the 'reading card' to monitor progress is emphasised, and parents are often invited to write comments, so entering into a dialogue on progress with the teacher. Usually booklets are provided so that parents can refer back to these as the project progresses. Enthusiasts for this approach claim twice the normal rate of progress.

The PACT (Parents, Children and Teachers) work in Hackney described by Griffiths and Hamilton[3] follows this pattern. Other examples are to be found in the Bellfield Project in Rochdale and the Harringay Project, both of which have been reported extensively; more details can be found in Bloom (1987)[4.]

Prepared reading

With this approach the parent and the child talk about the book before the reading session starts. The conversation can include a summary of the book so far, trying to guess what happens next or simply a discussion about the illustrations.

The parent then reads the book, the child silently reads the same piece and then reads aloud with prompting from the parent when needed.

Paired reading

In paired reading the parent reads a passage of a book to their child, then the parent and the child read the same passage together with the parent providing the error words.

Sometimes parents are encouraged to fade out their contribution as the child gains confidence but join in again if the child experiences difficulties. A useful book on paired reading is *Parental Involvement in Children's Reading* by Keith Topping and Sheila Wolfendale.[5]

Fund-raising

Like it or not, schools need the financial support of parents to provide an acceptable standard of equipment and materials to match the needs of the curriculum. The HMI report, *LEA Provision for Education and the Quality of Response in Schools and Colleges in 1985,* shows that more than 5% of primary schools gained at least twice as much as their capitation allowance through voluntary fund-raising activities. The developments under Local Management of Schools will not make schools less reliant on voluntary contributions.

Some schools have no problems in raising money. The parents are willing and able to dig deep into their pockets to finance the most ambitious schemes. However in less advantaged areas, schools are well aware of the financial hardship of many families, and are reluctant to put even more pressure on limited resources. After all, it is more important that children are adequately clothed and fed, than a new computer or hall curtains are bought for the school.

In the search for money-raising ideas we need to be aware of the image that we are projecting to the parents and community. Too often the the message that we give is that when children are not engaged in some form of 'trivial pursuit' — cramming objects into match boxes, wearing funny noses or wearing their clothes back to front, then they are engaged in some form of pre-Victorian drudgery evidenced by sponsored spell, sponsored tables test and sponsored silence.

Fund-raising is an important issue, but it is not really the main purpose of the school. If parents are willing to undertake responsibility for organising money-making activities then that leaves teachers with more time to concentrate on curriculum issues. When parent organisations raise money for the school then it certainly seems right for the parents' organisation to have some say in the way that the money is spent.

Parents helping at school

There is an accepted wisdom that having parents in schools during the working day is a good thing to do; that extra pairs of adult hands are always valuable around the school. The range of activities in which parents become involved range from re-painting book cases, with little contact with children, to active involvement in the teaching and supervision of children in small group work. It's very easy to drift into a system of parental involvement by accident, a system that just seems to work and be a part of the school which never gets reviewed or seriously challenged. After all who in their right mind looks gift horses in the mouth? Schools that take this attitude and don't review their strategies of parental involvement on a fairly thorough and frequent basis leave themselves wide open for all sorts of problems. Those parents that are not involved in school can harbour suspicions that some form of favouritism exists and that those involved in and around the school are a 'clique' that exerts power in obtaining preferential treatment for their own children to the disadvantage of others. On the other hand, those parents involved in helping in school can feel that their good will is being abused and that they are little more than washers of paint pots and menders of books. Staff too can be negative, taking the view that there is enough to do in school without having pushy parents under foot.

There is sometimes concern about the confidentiality of parent helpers; this can often be apparent in the way that parent helpers are treated at break-times. When parent helpers take their breaks in classrooms or hall then hidden and perhaps even quite open messages are given.

Some of the following questions should be considered in any review of parent helping at school:

1. *What can be gained from parents helping at school?*
   Creating a greater understanding of what school is about?
   Freeing teachers from time-consuming domestic tasks such as tidying, cleaning and repairing equipment?
   Extra pairs of hands for supervision of small group work?
   Expert instruction for children in specific skill areas such as cookery, craft, sport?
   Extra ears to listen to children read?
2. *How should parent helpers be chosen?*
   By invitation from the head?
   By invitation from individual teachers?
   By an appeal for volunteers addressed to all parents?
   What steps are taken to ensure the involvement of a cross-section of parents from the community that the school serves?
   Should all offers of help be accepted?
   How can you check on suitability? There have been instances, fortunately rare, where children have been assaulted at school by parent helpers. Has the LEA or the school any way of checking that parent helpers have no criminal record involving child abuse?
3. *Where should parent helpers work?*
   In the classroom alongside the teacher?
   In the corridor outside the classroom just listening to readers (the good ones? The poor ones? What sort of help? What sort of feedback to the teacher?)
   In an area of the school that is not overlooked by a member of staff?
   Should staff have a choice in the parents that work with them?
   Should parents have a choice of teacher that they help?
   Should parents help their own children?
4. *When should parent helpers work?*
   When they feel like popping into school?
   Should they follow a fixed timetable?
5. *What should happen to parent helpers at breaktimes?*
   Should they have their breaks in the staff room or is this an intrusion into staff freedom?
   Should they have their break in the classroom with the classteacher?
   Should they have their break with the head?
   Should they be abandoned to fend for themselves?
   Should they be asked to make a contribution to the tea fund?

6. *What sorts of activities are legitimate for parents to tackle at school?*
   Odd jobs in the classroom?
   Maintenance tasks such as painting and decorating, plumbing and wiring?
   Kept at some sort of curriculum fringe, involved in art, sewing, cookery but not science, maths or language work?
   Or using their specialist skills to teach children?

7. *Should parent helpers have some form of training?*
   If so, who should provide it? The head? The staff? Other parents? The LEA?
   What form should it take?

8. *What sort of protection is provided for parents?*
   In the event of an accident to a parent helper or to a child being supervised by a parent helper what could be the legal consequences? What sort of protection does the LEA or the Parents' Association offer?

Everyone taking part and everyone winning a prize needs to be the basis of good mutual support between parents and schools. There will always be parents that provide a great deal of time and energy to the school and there will be others who, with the best will in the world, can only provide the minimum of practical support. No matter what level of commitment can be offered, no-one should feel excluded or feel that they and their children are at a disadvantage. Positive change and development occurs when there is trust and co-operation between all partners.

Schools that put themselves out to work with parents do it at a cost of time and effort. There is no quantitive way of measuring the effectiveness of this input. Even if there are measurable gains in pupil numbers, knowledge and skills levels of pupils or even in school funds there is no way of knowing whether, if the time and effort spent on working with parents had been directed along other channels, then even better results would have been obtained.

Working with parents to improve pupil performance just seems the most natural way of primary schools to operate. It is often demanding, frequently frustrating; but is always rewarding and well worth the effort.

References

1   Wolfendale, S. (1985) 'A framework for action: professionals and parents as partners' in De'Arth, M. and Pugh, G. (eds) *Partnership Paper 1,* National

Children's Bureau, London.

2   ILEA (1985) *Improving Primary Schools*, Report of the Committee of Inquiry chaired by Norman Thomas, London.

3   Griffiths, A. and Hamilton, D. (1984) *Parent Teacher, Child*, Methuen. London.

4   Bloom, W. (1987) *Partnership With Parents in Reading*, Hodder and Stoughton.

5   Topping, K. and Wolfendale, S. (1985) *Parental Involvement in Children's Reading*, Croom Helm.

8 New initiatives in primary maths

Ruth Merttens

Aspects of Primary Education: The teaching and learning of Mathematics: A Report by HMI (HMSO 1989) clearly shows that although mathematics in the majority of primary schools takes up a great deal of curriculum time the quality of learning that takes place is often very disappointing. Ruth Merttens has long advocated that parents can play an important role in maths teaching and through her work with the IMPACT (Maths for Parents Teachers and Children) project has successfully demonstrated ways and means of creating and harnessing parental involvement. The National Curriculum obliges schools to provide parents with quite detailed information on their children's progress in a variety of curriculum areas including mathematics. In this chapter Ruth Merttens strongly argues that teachers' accountability is not enough and can, in many ways, be unintentionally misleading. Outlined are ways in which schools can actively involve parents in their children's learning of mathematics and through this process help parents gain valuable insights into their children's progress.

Teachers are at this moment facing a period of rapid change in education. Indeed the scale of the change implied by the Education Reform Act can scarcely by exaggerated. The reactions to the imposition of the National Curriculum in the teaching profession and in primary classrooms up and down the country have been mixed. On the one hand there are still those who believe that to panic about the situation is to over-react, and that basically we shall all be able to continue much as we were before. Little, they feel, will in fact alter. At the other extreme, there is a pessimistic view of an educational world in which all children are labelled from the age of five, and in which schools and even classrooms are judged by their distributions of results. In this scenario, teaching has become largely a process of instruction and the curriculum is as limited as the pedagogy used to deliver it.

The implementation of the National curriculum will alter both teaching practices and the expectations of the learners and their parents. The precise form of these changes is not yet fixed, and to an extent at least, the actions of teachers during the next two years will affect the final shape of the education which we are to inherit. It is therefore more important than at any other time in recent educational history that we have a clear idea of which new initiatives will assist us. We must not only deliver the National Curriculum but also ensure that its delivery maintains and instigates the approach to children's learning and to education which we wish to see.

National Curriculum delivery

The National Curriculum incorporates three major changes in primary education.

1. Accountability

The National Curriculum has been described as 'accountability gone mad'. The reporting back of the assessment results, coupled with the requirements of ERA as regards the provision of information about programmes of study and schemes of work, will supply the consumers in education with comparative data never before available.

Parents are entitled to have access to the relevant Programme of Study and also to the more detailed teacher's Scheme of Work for their own individual child. This must include details of which attainment targets in each subject are to be attempted and at what levels. Parents must be told of any assessments occurring during the year, including the details of any Standard Assessment Tasks. They will have a right to be informed as to the outcome of all assessments, and this information about their individual child must be related to comparative information about the class as a whole. The outcomes of assessments are likely to be discussed with parents in terms of Profile components rather than Attainment Targets, but it is recommended by NCC that teachers should allow parents access to their records of each child's progress on each attainment target.

2. Specified educational objectives

The Statements of Attainment serve two functions. They are the specified 'Staged Criteria' against which the level of achievement of each pupil can be monitored. Thus they have an essential role to play in assessment. But they also represent educational objectives to be borne in mind when planning and teaching. An Attainment TARGET is something for which one aims. Teachers must now plan and deliver the National Curriculum by referring constantly to these objectives.

The dual nature of the Statements of Attainment as simultaneously portions of the curriculum CONTENT and criteria for ASSESSMENT has allowed some confusion to develop in the minds of many teachers. However, there is no doubt that from now on all teachers are going to have to plan their curriculum by making explicit references to the relevant Attainment Targets. There will be a strong tendency therefore to teach *to* these objectives. This is made more likely when put alongside the requirements concerning the information re-Schemes of Work to which parents are now entitled.

3. National Curriculum process = assessment

With or without SATs, the National Curriculum can be described as one giant assessment process. The CONTENT of the curriculum is now divided into 10 levels of attainment. This means that whenever a child is given a piece of work, a task or an activity to get on with, that activity or task etc. is itself calibrated or at least calibratable against the National Curriculum as laid out in the Statutory Orders. Therefore if we study a child's record of all the activities in, for example, maths which he has attempted over the last half term, we will obtain a partial assessment of that child. If Fred has done three level 1 activities and 25 level 2 activities and four level 3 activities, then we can anticipate that he is likely to emerge as a child who has attained (so far) level 2 in that particular subject.

For the first time, teachers' records of the 'hands-on' experiences of a child will be an explicit part of the assessment of that child's level of achievement. It has perhaps always been true that there is no teaching without assessment, but it has never before been the case that explicit assessments were based upon teachers' judgements of what tasks a child should do in class. This is a direct effect of dividing the CONTENT of the curriculum into levels for ASSESSMENT purposes.

Particular issues in primary mathematics

The last 10 or so years have seen some far-reaching changes in the traditional approaches to the teaching of mathematics to primary aged children. There is an increasing emphasis upon practical activities and a view of problem-solving as lying 'at the heart of mathematics'.[1] There is a desire to teach as much of the maths curriculum as possible through a more integrated and topic-based approach. These have characterised the post-Plowden, post-Cockcroft initiatives in primary mathematics. However, although many teachers have been convinced of the value of the prevailing orthodoxies, the parents have remained to a large extent both uninformed and unimpressed.

1.   Parent vocabulary versus teacher vocabulary

Over the last 20 years 'good' teaching practice in the primary school has increasingly depended upon a post-Piagetian view of the child as 'an active enquiring discovering learner who develops at his own pace'.[2] Knowledge has come to be defined in terms of experience and activity — 'As concepts to be acquired not facts to be stored'.[3] Such constructions of the 'developing child' contribute to a 'normalisation of what mother-child interaction consists of and a new orthodoxy in what constitutes the role of the mother'.[4]

Thus parents and teachers have developed divergent and, to some extent, isolated vocabularies within education. This has repercussions for the effectiveness of any communication between the two groups and for their separate construction of non-mutual assumptions. For example, a teacher may refer to an activity or task as being 'only skills practice'. In teacher vocabulary this indicates that the activity is limited in what it requires of the child. It also carries overtones of a dull or unimaginative pedagogy and a restricted curriculum. In parent vocabulary the word skill suggests competence and successful application. Practice is seen as a necessary part of the acquisition of skills. A skilled person is to be admired. Good teaching instructs in the acquisition of skills as far as possible.

More seriously, the communication gap emerges when teachers and parents are discussing a child's assessment results. A teacher may inform parents that a child is 'doing very well' or 'learning very effectively' in a particular subject. They may feel that a child has made good or moderate progress. However, in the teacher's mind, none of these comments are incompatible with the fact that this particular child is well behind where we might expect her to be, and will not in fact be likely to succeed in passing external examinations. A teacher is giving an assessment based not upon a comparison of the girl with her peer group in that school, or with some 'notional' average performance. They are comparing the girl's achievement with her own past performance. But what a parent HEARS in this situation is not likely to be what the teacher wishes to SAY. The parent will understand from such a report that their child is likely to do very well on any external examinations, and that they are well up with their peer group.

There is frequently a dichotomy between the assumptions and vocabulary of teachers and those of parents. This, particularly with a view to the satisfactory delivery of the National Curriculum, must be an issue which we address as a matter of urgency.

2. Transference of skills

There is now considerable evidence that one of the problems in mathematics is that children fail to transfer the skills that they acquire in the classroom to the 'outside' world of the street, the market place or the home. Margaret Donaldson[5] has demonstrated that it is not simply the context in which children operate that makes them feel more or less comfortable and therefore correspondingly more or less likely to perform well. Rather, the context must be seen as an integral part of what is being demanded of the child.[6]

We see the effects of this when we observe children failing to perform some mathematical technique in a situation at home, even though they can apply their knowledge perfectly adequately in a particular and familiar situation at school. Mary Harris[7] has noted how adolescents fail to transfer skills acquired at school to the workplace, and, more importantly, fail to make the connections between the skills they are using at work, and those they were taught at school. Martin Hughes[8] also finds evidence of similar failures in young children.

It is obviously necessary that children DO transfer mathematical skills from one context to another. The power of mathematics comes precisely from the ability to be able to generalise — 3 + 3 = 6 is as true if you are dealing with beads threaded on to a string in the classroom as it is if you are counting mugs of tea at home. With the increased emphasis upon skills acquisition in the National Curriculum it is important that the teaching of mathematics is seen to enable children to succeed in applying their knowledge in a variety of situations.

3.   Relation between INSET and changing classroom practice

Many in-service initiatives have occurred since the publication of the Cockcroft report. There has been an emphasis upon classroom-focused INSET, since it has been widely held that the most effective way to change a teacher's practice is to work alongside her in the classroom.

However, some have felt that trying to bring about new initiatives in primary mathematics is not unlike attempting to alter the shape of a piece of 'live' dough by sticking one's fingers into it. To start with there is a satisfactory dent in the dough, but over a period of time the dough fills out the holes and slowly but surely resumes its former shape. This is because, as Patrick Easen points out, 'Real change, as opposed to superficial or short-term changes, are often a result of a ... paradigm change. They rarely happen without it'.[9]

What is required in terms of instigating and establishing new initiatives in the classroom is a means of ensuring that any changes in practice are maintained. It is also helpful if the practice is permanently monitored by someone who has an interest in maintaining those changes.

Parental involvement

In the late '70s and early '80s, following the Dagenham Research Project[10], there were a number of initiatives in which efforts were made to secure sustained parental involvement in their children's learning to read. The results of such projects as the Harringay Project[11], the Coventry Community Education Project[12] and the

Pitfield Project in Hackney[13] were sufficiently startling to make large numbers of teachers and others involved in education sit up and take notice. As Dorothy Hamilton and Alex Griffiths wrote, 'We can now say with certainty, from the evidence of both research and practice, that where parents help consistently with reading, their children gain both in reading age and in the quality and enjoyment of their reading.'[14]

The Thomas Report[15] recommended that 'A scheme is set up and monitored in which parents are encouraged to become involved in their children's learning of maths'. IMPACT (Maths for Parents and Children and Teachers) ran as a pilot project in the ILEA from 1985 to '86. In 1987 IMPACT was set up as a large educational research and intervention initiative running in three authorities; Redbridge, Barnet and Oxfordshire. From 1989 onwards the IMPACT Project has involved schools in more than 15 LEAs across England and Wales.

How IMPACT works

The IMPACT process is best depicted on a diagram, as in Figure 1. Each week the teacher selects or designs a mathematical activity for the children to take home and share with their parents and/or siblings. The results of the work done at home are brought back and feed into or help to construct the following week's classwork. Examples of IMPACT activities include:

Figure 1: Activities going home and feeding back into the classwork

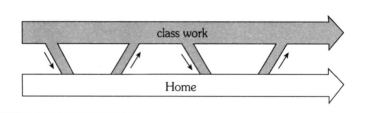

–   those which involve some sort of data collection or the bringing in of information from the home (see Figure 2).

Figure 2

Unit Search

What sort of units are used to tell you how much of something you are buying?

Go round a shop. Look at food.

How many units can you find?

Here are some, can you add others?

Unit	What it's measuring	Comment
gram		
ounce		
pound		
ml.		
cc.		

—   those which involve making or doing something at home (see Figure 3).

Figure 3

Draw a Map!

Can you draw a map of one place that you have walked to this weekend?

Include things like special buildings, post boxes, sign posts, telephone kiosks, railway lines, bridges, and any other things you notice.

Note to Parents
The children will need a lot of help drawing their maps. Some maps may be very simple and not look much like a "real" map. This does not matter. Encourage children to think about left and right and which way they have to turn.

–   those which involve practising a skill or reinforcing a mathe-
    matical idea (see Figure 4).

Figure 4

Divide and Cover

You will need 2 dice and some
counters. Each player needs
a 5 × 5 square grid, filled in
with a random arrangement of
numbers from 0 to 9.

Take turns throwing the dice,
which are then read as a two
digit number. Place a counter
on any number on your grid
which can be divided into the
two digit number.

So, if you throw a 2 and a 1,
you may cover any number
that can be divided into 21,
i.e. 1 or 3 or 7.

The winner is the first player
to either cover all of their
grid, (for a shorter game the
winner must get four counters
in a straight line).

The advantages of this way of working are:

- The teacher must relate all the maths done in the classroom to the maths that occurs at home and as a part of daily life.
- The children also relate their school work to the home context with all the advantages in terms of the transference of skills that this implies.
- Practical tasks, allowing children to solve problems and to develop individual strategies, become a major part of every teacher's classwork.
- The parents are involved on a weekly basis in sharing mathematical activities with their children. The resulting dialogue between home and school, teacher and parent is extremely helpful in building and maintaining a real working partnership.

IMPACT has been well described elsewhere,[16] and although the process remains the same, the finer details of the classroom practice vary from school to school and even, to a lesser extent, from classroom to classroom. It is often said by teachers or by advisers that they feel that they are not yet ready to involve the parents in the curriculum. They express a desire to 'get the maths right first'. Richard Border[17] has remarked that he would have no objection to schools keeping the parents out while they sort out the curriculum as long as they also keep the children out. The point here is that parents ARE involved in their children's education whether teachers choose to acknowledge this or not.

Effects of structured parental involvement on the issues outlined above

1.   Parent vocabulary versus teacher vocabulary

Involving the parents in the learning process in a structured and regular manner quickly assists the development of a common vocabulary for teacher/parent dialogue.

1.1   *Listening to parents*

Because of the regular and frequent nature of the contact involved, teachers will listen to parents' comments, both about their own particular child's learning and about the classroom maths curriculum in general. The importance of such listening cannot be over-rated. Richard Border (ibid.) describes how, as a headteacher, he opened his school up to parents. They had curriculum meetings, they encouraged parents to work in the classrooms alongside teachers, he himself kept an open-door policy so that he was easily available to parents. However, at the end of his time in that school as headteacher, a parent came in to complain. He explained that he didn't think that parents were taken seriously. Upon Richard's indignant denial of this, he replied, 'Oh yes, we can come in and talk to you any time we like. You will always discuss any aspect of the school we like. But you never really LISTEN and nothing ever really changes'.

The schools in which it has been hardest to develop a constructive and effective dialogue and subsequent partnership between parents and teachers are those in which the teachers are most confident that they have 'got the maths curriculum right'. In a situation where teachers hold rigidly to the prevailing orthodoxy in maths education they are less likely either to adapt their teaching because of parental demand or to recognise any defects as being attributable to their approach.

It was found on IMPACT that parents persistently reported that the activities sent home were 'too easy'. Much discussion and speculation has taken place about this result and there is not the space to do justice to the complexity of this finding here.[18] However, once the process of working with parents is established within a particular teacher's pedagogy, the parents' comments and suggestions become less threatening and can genuinely open a discussion about the directions in which the maths curriculum should move. Thus parents will accept the need for practical activities much more readily if they are the weekly witnesses of the child's difficulty in grasping some mathematical idea or acquiring a particular skill. Similarly, teachers will accept that a demand for more written recording may be reasonable in a situation where the children are seeing the practical applications of mathematics in the home.

1.2   Teachers to explain and account for practice

The result of sending home weekly activities for parents and children to share is that at the regular parent meetings teachers are frequently asked what the point of a particular activity is, and why they have done a particular sequence of activities. Teachers are being required to account for their teaching practice and their coverage of the curriculum in more detail than ever before. As mentioned above, with the National Curriculum, this demand takes on the status of a legal requirement.

It became imperative on IMPACT that the planning process itself became a part of the system of involving parents in these ways. Teachers plan a half-term or a term's maths. Many teachers take the opportunity to plan their whole curriculum for that period in an integrated fashion.

It is clearly not going to be possible to deliver the National Curriculum, all 70+ Attainment Targets, without some degree of integrated work and so teachers who have become used to planning in these ways have achieved in a short space of time a certain confidence with this way of working. More detail is given in *How to Deliver the National Curriculum — A Survivor's Guide*[19] about the precise steps involved in planning a scheme of work.

1.3   Using the same vocabulary

When activities are going home as a part of normal classroom routines, both teachers and parents become used to the weekly discussions which surround these. Children explain 'school' terminology to parents — 'My Mum has never heard of 'tesselations' so I had to show her'. Parents have a reason to question things which are not clear. Teachers find themselves thinking about where the particular area of maths with which they are dealing relates to the mathematics of 'everyday life'.

The National Curriculum is intended to supply one common vocabulary for teachers, parents, and anyone else concerned in education to use. Within three or four years it is envisaged that we shall all be speaking in terms of levels and attainment targets and profile components.

1.4   Acquiring mathematical skills

One result of sending home weekly maths activities and tasks is that parents see and appreciate the struggle their child may have with some parts of the maths curriculum. They may come to appreciate that a particular task is not as easy as it looks, or that something that they thought was obvious may be anything but obvious to a small child! Parents have often commented on how long it has taken them to help a child perform an activity which they had assumed was simplicity itself. One parent said that she had never realised how difficult it was to measure a bed using a handspan! Another parent described how trying to number a simple track had nearly driven her and her son mad! She said that she would not have believed how different numbering a track was from being able to 'count', i.e. chant the numbers in order.

Some of the tasks and activities which children take home each week are genuinely new to parents, being either part of mathematics which they did not do at school or having been forgotten since the leaving of school and throwing away of maths books. In these cases, the children and the parents may gain a great deal from working through a task as equals.

2.   Transference of skills

It is in this area that structured home-involvement schemes such as IMPACT really pay dividends. Teachers can sometimes be surprised how difficult it is to relate the maths they are doing in the classroom to any practical activity or application outside the school. This means that they can perceive parts of the maths curriculum in a different and perhaps more critical light. When sending activities home certain things must be remembered as listed below.

2.1   Children's performances at home

In Gordon Well's research on The Bristol Language Development Project, the differences between home and school were striking. Detailed samples of children's conversation at home provided Wells with a vast data pool which could be analysed to pull out those features of parental speech which seem to be associated with the children's rate of development. Newson in 1978[20] has pointed out that 'it is only because mothers impute meaning to "behaviours" elicited from infants that these eventually do come to constitute meaningful actions as far as the child himself is concerned'. Wells argues that learning is essentially an interactive process, that it is in the joint negotiation of meaning that learning and the acquisition of language takes place. 'In the pre-school years, conversation is most effective when it is collaborative, when it is a joint construction'.[21]

Parents, then, supply a constant range of interactive episodes.

The dominant style of interaction in school tends to be a teacher-dominated and interrogation-like form of speech. By contrast, parents tend to produce language which is ideally matched to the shared focus of attention. By the time children come to school they have learned a very great deal and they have done so as active 'meaning-makers'. They were supported at home by parents who followed their interests, encouraged their initiatives, and tried to help them develop and extend their range of skills. The children's learning at home, however, because it is spontaneous, is 'sporadic, unsystematic, and to a considerable extent, idiosyncratic'. Wells comments that 'there are undoubtedly many teachers who interact with children in this way, collaborating with them in their meaning-making, whilst at the same time...helping them to extend their understanding further. However, it seems from our observations that this is the exception rather than the rule'.

Children's learning at home, then, is quite different from the learning which takes place in school. At home, children behave in entirely different ways and are capable of quite different things. As we know from the Bristol Language Development Project, two activities which appear to require the same skills are in fact requiring quite different sets of skills if the context for one is home and for the other, school. A good example of this is given by comparing the following two questions. As a teacher in school I say, 'How many beads have you got on that string?'. The child knows that I am not asking for information. They know that I know the answer to this question. Certain strategies are acceptable in enabling them to answer this question and others are not. It is perfectly acceptable to count. It is unacceptable to ask a friend for help. If I am at home and, as a mother I shout through to the kitchen, 'And how many biscuits are left in the tin for Daddy?', the children know that I am asking for information. They also know that certain strategies are OK — for example, one might turn to an older brother and ask, 'How many have we left?', or one might lie! Although the questions appear superficially to be the same, the context in which they occur makes them quite different and means that different sets of skills may be employed in answering them.

It is very difficult for teachers to predict how children will perform when doing a particular activity at home. As many IMPACT activities as possible need to be 'elastic'. They will span several levels of attainment according to how far you take them (see Figure 5). This means that children can take an activity as far as they feel is comfortable. It also means that one activity can be sent to a class containing a number of children who are at widely differing levels of achievement.

Figure 5

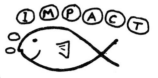

Sum and Product Game

You will need someone to play
with. You can use a calculator
if you like.

One of you thinks up 2
numbers (you can use
decimals).

Multiply them together...............
.... (this is the product).

Add them together ....
.... (this is the sum).

Now tell your partner the
product and the sum.

Your partner has to guess
what your secret numbers
are!

Your partner gives you one to
do at the same time.

Who guesses first?

How many numbers did you
try?

2.2   Peer tutoring

Each week the children take home a sheet of paper on which is outlined the activity they are expected to share with their parents or cousins or siblings or Granny or someone at home. The piece of paper, however, is not the principal vehicle by which the activity is shared. The main source of instruction is the child. The child carries the information as to what must happen at home and then instructs the adults. The usual adult/child tutor/tutee dynamic is therefore reversed. The child acts as the tutor. The adult, who may not understand the task at all, and certainly is not the one who was there when it was explained, must listen to the child and be 'tutored'.

This provides a particular case of 'peer tutoring'. It means that the child is regularly required to construct and explain mathematical tasks given at school in the home context. The cognitive effort needed to perform this function week after week results in an increase in mathematical competence in this area. As one teacher reported, 'After a year of doing IMPACT there was a noticeable development in the ability of the children to explain rules or processes'. It would be surprising if this were not the case since, as Keith Topping notes,[22] 'conditions conducive to the development of responsive and independent learning include the fact that the learner must be able in INITIATE rather then merely react to stimuli controlled by another, and ... also that there is a reciprocity or mutual influence with each participant modifying the behaviour of the other'.

Teachers have also reported that children show an increased awareness of examples of mathematics which occur in the world around them. For example, one six-year-old child when walking along the street was heard to remark, 'That's measured in litres. We do all about them in school'. Many parents have expressed a similar surprise at the increased number of occasions where mathematical ideas are explicitly mentioned. The talk which can be generated by an IMPACT activity at home is frequently of great assistance in enabling children to assimilate mathematical ideas and make them their own (see Figure 6).

A parent's written comments on this activity read 'We thought that both the cylinders were bound to hold the same since they were made from the same piece of paper. However, when we tried it we found that the short fat one held more than the tall thin one. Thinking cornflakes perhaps not really a very good measure (too much air space!) we tried the activity again with Persil. The short fat one still held more! HELP!?' It takes little imagination to see the benefits which could accrue from all the discussion involved in this activity at home.

Figure 6

<u>What's in a tube</u>?

You will need a cardboard
tube from a kitchen or toilet
roll, or a piece of card which
you can roll into a cylinder.

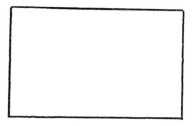

Place the cylinder on a plate
or dish, or on some
newspaper. Fill the cylinder,
carefully, with sand, or soil,
or rice.

Now empty out the contents,
and keep them aside. Now cut
the cylinder open, roll it the
other way and stick the join
with sellotape.
Fill this new
cylinder.
Does it hold the
same amount as
the other one?

3.   Maintaining changes vis à vis INSET support

IMPACT incorporates the following:

–   A form of 'peer-tutoring' whereby the child initiates the activity and instructs the adult or sibling participating.
–   A means whereby the mathematical skills and knowledge acquired in the classroom is applied to 'real life' situations.
–   The necessity for practical activities to be incorporated into all teachers' classwork.

The extent and scope of these changes to many traditional classroom practices would indicate that considerable difficulty could be expected in instigating such changes in such a way that they become a permanent feature of the IMPACT classroom. However, certain factors assist in this process as follows:

3.1   Materials-based

IMPACT is a materials-based project in the sense that it requires the teacher either to select from a large bank of suitable IMPACT materials or to design their own activity each week. The process relies upon an activity or task being taken home and the results of it feeding into the following week's work. While the materials exist and are used, the changes in practice to some extent follow automatically.

It is essential that the activity which goes home each week arises out of the mathematics that the children are doing in class. It is also important that the activity is one which the children will find enjoyable. Sometimes even practising a skill can be camouflaged as a game and can prove great fun to adults and children (see Figure 7).

Unlike the shared reading initiatives, the fact that something goes home and comes back into the classroom means that it is very difficult for a teacher's classwork not to be affected. A teacher may choose to ignore the passage of reading books to the home and back again. However, she is unlikely to ignore 30 potatoes when the children bring them in! (see Figure 8.)

Figure 7

Cash Check

You need a bank of money.
1. Each player starts with
25p.
2. Take turns throwing the
dice and moving along the
board.
3.   If you land on a white
square take the amount shown
from the bank.   If you land on
a shaded square, pay the
amount shown to the bank.
4.   The winner is the one with
the most money when someone
finishes.

16 2p Finish	15 1p	14 5p	13 1p
9 5p	10 1p	11 2p	12 1p
8 1p	7 5p	6 1p	5 2p
1 1p Start	2 2p	3 1p	4 5p

Figure 8

ⒾⓂⓅⒶⒸⓉ

<u>HEAVY POTATO!!</u>

Bring in the heaviest potato
you can find.
Fill in as many names as you
can on the diagram below
Heavier than my potato.

About the same as my potato.

Lighter than my potato.

<u>HINT TO PARENTS</u>
Select some things to write
on these diagrams that we
can check in school— e.g. a
sock, a shoe, a pencil..........

3.2   Parent pressure

Once activities have been sent home for a while, the parents start to become accustomed to their role in the partnership which develops.

– They now understand better what is going on in the classroom in terms of the maths curriculum.
– They have a sense of assisting their child's mathematical development.
– They feel that what they do at home has an effect on what happens in the classroom and vice-versa.
– They frequently enjoy the activities and have fun together!

If the teacher stops working in this way, the parents will complain. The pressure to maintain these changes is therefore increased.

Concluding remarks

Within IMPACT there are several new initiatives on how to approach the teaching of primary mathematics. A teacher or school could choose to adopt just one of the aspects mentioned in this chapter. Peer tutoring could be incorporated as a routine way of working. Asking children to notice applications of the maths they are studying in class could be a part of the work of any classteacher. Building in time for talking to parents on a regular basis about their children's learning in maths is often something which can be achieved through a careful structuring of teachers' time within a whole school.

The Education Reform Act has altered completely the context within which we teach. Given the scope and scale of the changes we are now facing in education it is important that we look to new initiatives to:

– assist us in the delivery of the National Curriculum
– enable us to teach in a child-centred fashion and to preserve autonomy with regard to classroom organisation.

Matters for urgent concern

1.   Assessment

The entire National Curriculum has been designed with assessment in mind. The content of the curriculum has been arranged in 10 levels of attainment and any aspect of a subject which could not be so arranged (e.g. practical applications in mathematics) has been left out or re-written to fit the assessment design.

Because of the way that the curriculum is arranged, coupled with the requirements for the reporting back of the outcomes of assessment, every time a teacher selects a piece of content — an activity — for a child, this selection will act as a partial assessment. For example, if I look along my class records and I see that Fred has done activities A,B,C,D, and E, I can look to see at what level on each Attainment Target each of these activities is calibrated. I can then state that Fred is currently performing at a particular level in maths, at least in the relevant Attainment Targets. This raises several serious questions:

1.1   The fallibility of teachers' judgements

Teachers' judgements when it comes to what children can do or are capable of doing are naturally fallible. There is evidence that teachers over-estimate confident mature children and under-estimate disruptive or immature children. A teacher might give a socially inept child a piece of work at level 1. He may fail to complete it or perform badly. The teacher may therefore present him with another piece of work at level 1 and so on. The teacher's selection of tasks will mean that such a child would probably come out on any continuous assessment as achieving at level 1. This could belie the fact that such a child could attain level 3 if given the opportunity.

One possible means of trying to minimise the damaging effects of teachers' misjudgements in such a system is to involve the parents not only in the learning process but also in the assessments as well. Several IMPACT schools have been trialling parent assessment. Termly assessment schedules are sent home based upon the work that the children and parents have shared through IMPACT (see Figure 9). These are completed by parents and teachers separately. Any major discrepancies then provide the starting point for a useful dialogue.

There is now ample evidence, from research and practice, of the damage that wrong judgements made by teachers can do to individual children.[23] We now have a system whereby daily choices made by teachers have cumulatively the effect of an official assessment. Any assistance to help minimise the risk of errors can only be to everyone's advantage.

Figure 9

ASSESSMENT SHEET   Lower Juniors   Spring Term 1989

Child's Name ...   .

SKILLS and FACTS	LEVEL	YES- understand NO/ NOT SURE
Understand that multiplication is a number of sets or groups all the same e.g. 4 X 3 = 4 lots of 3.		YES
Recognise which numbers are odd and which are even.	Up to 20	YES
	Up to 50	YES
	Up to 100	YES
Know which numbers up to 100 are square numbers and why they are so called.	up to 25 + knows number(s)	what a square number is
Can add two numbers together e.g. 10+5 25+21 62+37 a) mentally i.e. in their head. b) using pencil and paper.	Up to 50	a) YES b) YES
	Up to 100	a) YES b) YES
	Any numbers	a) NO YES BUT→ (with fingers)
Can subtract numbers e.g. 22-11 74-56 104 - 71 a) mentally. b) using pencil and paper.	Up to 50	a) NO b) NOT VERY
	Up to 100	a) No b) Well
	Any numbers	a) No b) No TRIES TO DO IT UPSIDE DOWN
Know their tables.	2 times table	YES
	3	Just about
	4	Almost
	5	YES
	6	No
	7	Some!
	8	No
	9	No
	10	YES
Can multiply 2 one-digit numbers in any way which gives the correct answer.	1 to 9 X 1 to 9	AND 11's DEPENDS ON THE NUMBERS!
Can multiply any two numbers together in any way which gives the correct answer.	1 to 9 X 10 to 49	GONE
	1 to 9 50 to 99	No
	1 to 9 X 100 to 999	No
Can add together coins.	Up to 50p	YES
	Up to £1	YES
	Up to £5	YES
Can add up simple bills.	Up to £1	YES
	Up to £5	ALMOST
Can work out change.	From 50p	YES FOR SUMS ENDING 5 + 10
	From £1 (D.0.)" "	" " " " " ..."
	From £5	SORT OF -SUMS ENDING 5 no
Can record amounts of money.	As pence e.g. 24p	YES
	As pounds and pence e.g. £0.24	YES (Also, for ex £12.42)
Share a number of objects equally between a number of people.	Up to 20	YES
	Up to 50	NO
	Up to 100	No

handwritten top margin (rotated): ON THE LEFT PLACE INSTEAD of UNITS - ALSO "CARRIES" WRONG DIGIT etc

handwritten right margin (rotated): CLAIRE OFTEN TRIES REPEAT ADDITION

handwritten bottom: Claire often confuses addition + multiplication

1.2 SATs and their effects

In the short term, the SATs will obviously be the focus of intense attention. It is clear that the form that they take will directly and powerfully affect the shape of the curriculum and its related pedagogy.

However, there is concern not about the effect of the SATs in the next five years but in the long term, over the next 15 or 20 years. Many educationalists fear that the stringent reporting-back arrangements, when coupled with open-enrolment, will mean that the SATs themselves change in certain directions. The demand for the assessment processes to be simple and easily visible may mean an adaptation over time of those parts of the curriculum which are hardest to assess. This could result in the SATs becoming more restricted in their sampling of Attainment Targets. This would itself produce a much more limited curriculum. Furthermore, there could be pressure upon the SATs to restrict themselves to the modes in which assessment is easier in traditional terms. This will also have repercussions in terms of encouraging a more traditional and limited approach to teaching. For example, there could be pressure to place a much heavier emphasis upon written recording than is currently the case.

2. Goal-oriented teaching

The temptation, because of the structure of the National Curriculum, is for teachers to adopt a much more goal-oriented approach to teaching than many have done in the past. There are currently a large number of teachers who rely upon a more intuitive approach. Experienced teachers, like mothers, can perform the necessary tasks, choose and adopt strategies, adapt and control situations almost entirely intuitively. When such teachers are asked to account for their practice, their accounts will frequently contain references to educational objectives or goals. However, the aiming at such targets or the seeking after those objectives does not in fact form a part of their explicit teaching approach, although it may be implicit. These are responsive, intuitive and experienced teachers.

The demand that accurate and complete records of all activities are kept, and that these activities and tasks are themselves National Curriculum calibrated, will militate against this type of intuitive teaching. A teacher who dreams up an activity on the spur of the moment in response to a piece of work a child has brought her, or a particular social situation in the classroom, is hardly likely to dream up the calibrations for it as well. She may not be at all aware which Attainment Targets it covers or at what levels. She probably has not thought of it with conscious educational objectives in mind. She has dreamt up the activity because it feels right to her at the time. Given experience and a real concern for the children in her care, the teacher is very likely right in believing that activity to be suitable. But producing activities or tasks in this way may not fulfil the requirements of the National Curriculum. It will make those who teach in this way feel vulnerable when the whole of teaching is being structured in such a way as to give priority to the teacher's ability to account for what she is doing.

Resources

For those interested in obtaining assistance with any aspect of the initiatives described in this chapter, the following list may help:

IMPACT — For further information regarding Packs of suitable materials, Courses and Starter Kits contact:
The IMPACT Project
School of Teaching Studies
Polytechnic of North London
Prince of Wales Rd,
London NW5 3LB

Schools who may wish to join the IMPACT National Network can obtain details from Deborah Curle, IMPACT Project, Tel:071-607 2798

Peer tutoring — Two useful books are:
The Peer Tutoring Handbook: Promoting Co-operative Learning, by Keith Topping, Croom Helm, 1988

Peer Tutoring, by Sinclair Goodlad and Beverley Hirst, Kogan Page, 1989

Parental involvement — Two useful books are:
Parent, Teacher, Child, by Dorothy Hamilton and Alex Griffiths, Methuen, 1984

Parents in School, by Ruth Merttens and Jeff Vass, Scholastic Press, 1988

Books on National Curriculum:
Parent's Guide — How to Survive the National Curriculum, by Ruth Merttens and Jeff Vass, Octopus, 1989

How to Deliver the National Curriculum in the Classroom, by Ruth Merttens and Jeff Vass, Heinemann, 1989

References

ERA : *Education Reform Act 1988*, HMSO.

1   *The Cockcroft Report*, 1982, HMSO.

2   Walkerdine, V. (1985) 'On the Regulation of Speaking and Silence', in *Language, Gender and Childhood*, Routledge & Kegan Paul.

3   The Plowden Report, *Children and their Primary Schools*, 1967, HMSO.

4   Urwin, C. (1984) 'Power Relations and the Emergence of Language', in *Changing the Subject*, Methuen.

5   Donaldson, M. (1978) *Children's Minds*, Fontana.

6   Merttens, R. and Vass, J. (1988) 'Special Needs in Maths' in Robinson and Thomas, (eds.), *Tackling Learning Difficulties*, Hodder & Stoughton.

7   Harris, M. (1986) *Maths in Work* DTI.

8   Hughes, M. (1986) *Children and Number*, Blackwell.

9.   Easen, P. (1985) *Making School-centred INSET Work*, Croom Helm.

10   Hewison, J. and Tizard, J. (1979) *Dagenham Research Project*.

11   Tizard, J., Schofield, W.N. and Hewison, J. (1982) *Harringay Reading Project*.

12   Coventry Community Education Project (1982).

13   Hamilton, D. and Griffiths, A. (1984) *The Pitfield Project*.

14   Hamilton, D. and Griffiths, A. (1984) *Parent, Teacher, Child*, Methuen.

15   The Thomas Report (1984) *Improving Primary Schools*, ILEA.

16a Merttens, R. and Vass, J. (1988) *Parents in Schools*, Scholastic Press.

16b Merttens, R. and Vass, J. (1987) Raising Money or Raising Standards' in *'Education 3–13'*.

16c Merttens, R. and Vass, J. (1987) 'The Cultural Mediation and Determination of Intuitive Knowledge and Cognitive Development' in Mjaavatn, E. (ed.). *Growing into a modern world*.

17   Border, R. (1985) Unpublished Thesis.

18   Merttens, R. and Vass, J. Forthcoming papers for BERA.

19   Merttens, R. and Vass, J. (1989) *How to Deliver the National Curriculum — A Survivor's Guide*, Heinemann.

20   Newson, J. (1978)'Dialogue and Development' in Lock, A., (ed.) *Action, Gesture and Symbol*, London Academic Press.

21   Wells, G. (1985) *Language, Learning and Education*, NFER/Nelson.

22   Topping, K. (1988) *A Handbook of Peer Tutoring*, Croom Helm.

23   Pye, J. (1988) *Invisible Children*, Oxford University Press.

9 Developing drama and art in primary schools

David Sheppard

In this chapter David Sheppard argues convincingly for the maintenance and development of the arts in enriching the curriculum of the primary school. He also offers support through a variety of examples of ways of capturing children's imagination and engaging them in purposeful learning through the powerful medium of drama and art.

I believe in starting close to home. Here is a fragment of the transcript of a piece of 'drama' which took place in my living room recently:

Sam: Shall I take you to the pub?
Dad: Yes please.
Pause
Sam: Oh dear.
Dad: What's the matter?
Sam: Won't start.
Dad: Oh. What can we do?
Sam: Phone the ... man.
Dad: The AA?
Sam: Yes. The AA
Dad: O.K. You go and phone then. Tell them your address and say the car won't start.

Sam is three years old and of course I don't know where he gets his ideas from. What I do know is that this fiction is important to him in a variety of ways. I'm not sure whether it's as parent or teacher or mixture of both that I do it, but I try to fathom why he wants to take part in this activity — to guess 'what's in it for him'. Firstly, I think it's important to him to be involved in a narrative, or call it a plot, if you like. The events unfold in a pattern and a sequence that *he* controls. It belongs to *him*. It is *his* story. In this story, he is able to reverse a hierarchy that he usually encounters: in other words, *he* is in charge of *me*, *he* is responsible for *my* care. Interestingly, he does not choose for himself a smooth, trouble-free flow of developments. In fact, there is one problem after another, introduced into the narrative to temporarily block the progression of events. This strikes me as a kind of assertion of health: he demonstrates to himself that he knows problems do arise, and also that there are solutions to them. All of this is couched in a structured rehearsal or practice. He is developing for himself an increasing ability to play — of course he knows *really* that I am his dad and not his mate from work, that the car is not *really* a car but the settee, and probably even that the AA in real life take longer than 15 seconds to arrive. It is the fact that he knows these things but chooses to behave as if he knew otherwise that gives him access to the activities described above. If you like, it is a releasing agent which opens the door to advantages he provides for himself.

So why am I involved? What's in it for me? For one thing I manage to provide him with some basic information. He knows that when your car breaks down there is someone you can phone and I use the opportunity to apply a correct name to the concept he has already formed. (My apologies to other motoring organisations.) There's more than that in it for me, of course. We moved house recently, and Sam has been learning to say his new address. I take the opportunity within this make-believe to find out how he's getting on. If he tells the 'AA' over the phone the correct address I will know that he has sufficiently absorbed an aspect of his learning elsewhere for it to have become transferable to this very different situation, this very different mode of behaviour. Thus, for me, our pretence serves a diagnostic purpose.

Of course, the transcript gives you about as much as I can remember — the actual activity went on for much longer than is illustrated here, but in case you think I'm about to make exaggerated claims for something which, after all, took place in the early hours of the morning, now consider some of the opportunities I missed. In my own defence, let me say that at least I'm being honest, and in any case, I tend to be rather better at this sort of thing when I'm awake. I could, however, have done something about his assumption that only men fix cars. (For all the effort in this area that has taken place in our house, we still managed to produce a boy who wants to be an engine driver, on the grounds that he doesn't want to end up stuck in the kitchen like his father.) Looking back at the transcript fragment, I realise that this must have at least flickered across my brain at the time. I turn the AA as 'the man' into the non-committal 'them'. A signal of where I ought to have been, perhaps, but still a cop-out, all the same. As participant in the fiction I also have the opportunity to create the obstacles to our success, the problems we must solve, the possible choices as to what we should do next.

I didn't, in the fragment quoted, pay much attention to the extension of language usage — his vocabulary is augmented only by 'AA', the conversation is only in the form of the customary discourse between us and using the telephone is not new to him. Only later, when we practised ways of explaining to the AA man what had happened when we tried to start the car did anything start to happen in this area. Neither can it be claimed that there is any real engagement with the *aesthetic* — what I've been describing here is really an appropriation of some of the procedures of an art form in order to approach some aspect of education *through* the arts.

It's important to allow for things that could have occurred but didn't, because the teacher in us often has to make choices of emphasis on the spur of the moment and a different teacher makes a different choice. I've obviously been thinking about this incident because of the pointers it gave me toward what I feel about the ways the arts might feature in primary education: somewhere between these two massive areas of concern, 'what's in it for him' and 'what's in it for me' there exists a kind of negotiated common territory where we may meet without intruding upon the other's dignity. Across that territory a path meanders, sometimes nearer to 'what's in it for him', sometimes nearer to 'what's in it for me'. Sometimes the path is uphill and difficult, sometimes downhill and smooth. It is somewhere in the journey along this path that we may discover the vital contribution of the arts in education.

So how might this inform our thinking of what we would like to see happening in schools? How do these principles translate to setting up learning situations for whole classes of children? The concept of entering a fiction to negotiate areas of learning still applies, as does the creation of that peculiar kind of double-think — the state of tension between what one actually knows in real life, and what one pretends to know, or not know, within the drama. There are many approaches to drama in primary schools.

I am concentrating on only one of them. The fiction that we agree to enter can be derived from much of the existing business of our classroom: story corner, stories from history, other areas of the curriculum, personal anecdotes. It basically leans on the story, wherever it comes from, as a framework against which creative activity can be pitched. The children know the story, know the plot development already. The teacher's task becomes one of seeking 'points of intervention' in that narrative line in order to highlight, explore and deepen the children's understanding of the issues at stake.

Let's examine one example to see how this might work in practice. This particular story is about Krishna. Here are the bare bones of it:

> Krishna, fearing for his life, is in hiding from his wicked uncle, Kausa. Kausa summons up Kaliya, a seven-headed poisonous serpent and gives him instructions to find and kill Krishna. Kaliya swims up the River Jamuna and begins to terrorise the village where Krishna is in hiding. Eventually, Krishna appears, and begins to dance on the heads of the monster, rendering him tame, and sending him back to the depths of the ocean.

Let me first apologise for the great disservice I have done to this rich and powerfully dramatic story. My crude synopsis should, however, serve our present purpose. Once the class have fully absorbed the sequence of events, the basic story line, the teacher can identify an appropriate point of intervention. There are many available to us — I shall pick just one. This uses the drama technique of teaching in role. In this example the teacher adopts the role of a messenger, and approaches the class as if they were a meeting of the villagers. Teaching in role, is, of course, a highly developed technique and can require highly specialised skills. Now I think there are degrees of sophistication about the way in which this might actually be achieved. A reasonably accomplished practitioner would just begin the drama work, conveying the context to the class by the means of their own opening line. A class used to drama will be experienced in this kind of approach and accept this kind of procedure quite naturally. In other cases, if the class is not used to working in this way, or if the teacher lacks confidence, the scene may need to be set up, explained first. The important things to remember are that the work is still worth doing, even if one lacks skill in its exposition; that skills like this are, to a certain extent, gained by practice, anyway; and that the sensible thing is to set up the work in the way that suits you, and your class, on that particular day.

This scheme of work has now been very widely used. In quoting these possible examples, I have in mind a conglomerate of experiences of actual classroom use. Let's look at some of the circumstances of what we have set up here. The children find themselves in a drama which starts in the middle of the story as they know it. In other words, there is no question of them acting out the story from the beginning. (If we did that, they would be constantly thinking about what happens next, and I want them to think more deeply about what is happening now.) As it is, they know, in real life, all the events of the story — the people they will be in the drama know only some of them. Also, the scene I have set up does not actually occur in the story at all. There is no messenger, no meeting of the villagers. I have invented this scene and added it to the story in order to create a context for reflection on it. (I am particularly keen to do this when using stories which are religious, as I can therefore hope to avoid wrongly describing events which are a part of another person's personal faith.) These basic suggestions are best identified by quoting the teacher's 'opening line':

a. *'Excuse me, I've come from the next village. We heard you might be in some difficulty, and wondered if we could help'.* Perhaps the most stunning response I ever received to this one was 'Yes, we've run out of yoghourt'. I'm not proud. I stopped the drama, reminded the class that our drama was to be about the story of Krishna that we had heard that morning and started again. I don't regard this as failure — it's sometimes necessary to take a step backwards in order to take two forwards. On the vast majority of occasions, however, it hasn't taken long for the class to begin telling me about the monster that has invaded their village. Promptings like 'Monster? What kind of monster?' lead to a good deal of oral descriptive work before posing the real challenge: 'Come off it. I've had a long difficult journey over those mountains. Do you expect me to believe that? Is this some kind of practical joke?' This turns the focus of the work into a consideration of the *nature of proof.* I usually try to help channel this by referring to an external authority that will need to be convinced, usually the 'Head of the village'.

This opens up several opportunities for me as a teacher:

–   by being terribly contrite over my original response to the disaster that has befallen their village I can re-establish a seriousness and gravity to the situation.
–   the fact that I am but a humble messenger means that I can reasonably claim to know nothing, and thus place the power of knowledge in the hands of the class.

- by building up the picture of the head of my village, I can not only focus their efforts to convince on a particular audience, I can also build in an opportunity to question a role stereotype: 'the head of my village is an incredibly powerful and intelligent person. How are you going to convince her?' (This is also diagnostic. I am making a mental note of which children display surprise that the Head of a Village could be a woman.)
- this messenger doesn't have to be two dimensional. I have here an opportunity to present a man who is frightened, and thus offer an alternative role model to the macho style most commonly presented by the media.

The responses to this basic question of what constitutes proof tend to fall into categories:

- written. These sometimes take the form of personal letters, but more often are sworn statements, sometimes 'signed in blood'.
- visual. There have been times when the lesson has had to stop while we decide whether or not the villagers would have had cameras. Some teachers I have worked with choose to develop this work by having the class create the photographs/artist's impressions for themselves, others have encouraged the children to create the photographs using their own bodies, in 'frozen picture' style.
- by artifact. Skulls of animals or people killed by the monster are popular here, which prompted at least one teacher to embark on a lot of work with clay, looking at studies of heads. On other occasions, a sample of the serpent's venom has been suggested, leading another teacher to get the test tubes out and begin an extensive collection of 'samples' of all kinds of materials.

The point to be emphasised here is that whatever medium is chosen to communicate the 'proof', the children have a genuine purpose in undertaking the task (albeit a fictitious one into which they have voluntarily entered); they are writing to a defined audience, about whom an appropriateness of style has been identified and established; and their act of communication takes place within a recognisable context, outlined for them by the story's narrative but largely created for themselves. A rich vein of cross-curricular activity is contextualised by the drama framework. It's worth considering how a teacher might have set about achieving these results without using drama: 'Remember the story we heard about this morning. Imagine that you are one of the villagers and write a letter to someone in the next village, describing what has happened'.

b. *'Excuse me, I'm from the next village. We have a terrible problem, and wonder if you can help us.'* It's vital not to do this before example(a). If you do, you'll end up imposing *your* description of the monster on the rest of the class. This is also tantamount to an invitation to the class to get their own back — don't be surprised if they sneer in disbelief at your description of the serpent which is terrorising your village. There's an important difference, though. You are in the position of saying 'wait, I can prove it' and proceeding to distribute the pile of sworn statements signed in blood, or pictures, or test tubes full of venom that your fellow villagers have sent with you to back up your story. You will, of course, be using the actual work produced by the class in the lesson based on example (a). Thus, in this second role, the class have the opportunity to assess how convincing would be the work they have produced in their previous role. One teacher I worked with refined this process of self-assessment even further by ensuring that each child got back his or her *own* work. Additionally, this strategy allows some scope for satisfaction of the urge to develop the plot. Remember, the children *know* the solution to your problem: you get Krishna to dance on the monster's head. The interesting thing about it is that they very rarely tell you first off. They tell you third. Just as there are three billy goats gruff and three little pigs and it's the third pig who outsmarts the wolf, almost every class I have worked with come up with two poor suggestions, and only when they have been thrown out do they suggest the correct solution as defined by the storyline.

c. *'Excuse me, I seem to have lost my serpent'.* Watch out for absolute mayhem and only use this at all if you are completely sure of your class. When it works, it reveals a readiness to jump to conclusions. My most successful experience with it was short and angry, culminating in an outburst about my letting loose a 'seven-headed green thing that spat poison' which was silenced when I said: 'There must be some mistake. My serpent's orange.'

d. *'I believe you've been having trouble with a sea-monster. Is it green, seven heads, spits poison? Well, I'm his mother.'* This strategy is not original. I have seen Cecily O'Neill use it as the mother of the ogre in Jack and the Beanstalk. It capitalises on the shock of the thought that a monster might actually have a mother to crystallise this sudden seriousness of thinking into a consideration of the whole notion of social control. 'I've tried everything with that boy, given him everything. I tell him not to terrorise villages, he just takes no notice. What can I do?' This tends to explore the whole question of what discipline actually means. It's a peculiar state of affairs. The classes I have encountered, considering the behaviour of a mythical sea serpent, embarrassed at coming face to face with a male teacher who claims to be the serpent's mother, nevertheless suggest and discuss codes of conduct and the sanctions which reinforce them in terms which are very close to home. What they really talk about is the child who was naughty yesterday and had to sit in the head's room instead of doing games, yet they explore this intense social question in the relative safety of a context markedly distant in every respect of the word.

I have chosen these examples because they reflect a range of cross-curricular opportunities — there are many more which I do not have space to develop here. The work can be further enriched by the representations of this story in Indian Art, Music and Dance, for instance. Moreover, the work I have described is all from one 'point of intervention' in only one story, and these are only beginning points — there is considerable scope for further dramatic development, the opening up of more cross-curricular study, and, where appropriate, the selection and shaping of dramatic elements for presentation.

Recently, I was asked to detail how this kind of work might be useful in the implementation of the National Curriculum in English. I chose another well tried and tested example, but in highlighting the ways in which strategies can be devised to meet attainment targets described in the Cox Report, I cannot help but recall developments introduced by teachers I met in connection with my work as an Advisory Teacher in Inner London, and in many other parts of the country through the Arts in Schools Project. Much of this work can no longer be properly described as being anything to do with me.

The NCC non-statutory guidance for English points out: 'Pupils of all ages enjoy active imaginative play which provides the teacher with the basis for drama. Very young children enter into such play in the classroom, re-enacting school and home scenes and creating their own stories. The teacher is able to enter into such play, taking on a role which deepens the imagined experience and extends the children's use of language.'[1] The work centred on the story of Rumpelstiltskin. My own approach begins with a retelling of the story. There are several reasons for this. I want to give the children the experience of oral tradition that a storytelling rather than a story reading can offer. Although many of the children may have experienced the story before in some version or other, there may be other children in the class, particularly those from a different ethnic background, who may be unfamiliar with the story — a telling at the beginning of the work gives us a kind of definitive version from which we may begin our own creative explorations. Just as I am *using* the story (though hopefully in the best of causes) the story will have been *used* before. It is likely that a story like this one began life as a kind of coded cultural message in any case, and various versions since will have been constructed in line with particular sets of cultural mores. A telling gives me the opportunity to highlight what I call 'areas of question' in the story according to the needs, interests and desires of a particular group of children — not only the ones I expect to arise, by virtue of my previous knowledge of the class, but also those which emerge through the children's creative engagement with the material.

An approach I often use is to try and give the children a slant on the story from the point of view of a character in it; apparently forgotten characters are often particularly fertile ground. The villagers in Rumpelstiltskin are a good example — they 'appear' (by implication only) when we are told where the miller's daughter lives at the beginning of the story, and (in some versions) in celebratory mood when the wedding is announced and when the baby is born. In an attempt to suggest to the children that the story may be prominently about kings and queens but that ordinary people nevertheless have opinions too I introduce the element of concern on the part of the villagers during the three nights that the girl is spinning straw into gold, and insert into the story an occasion on which a group of villagers actually turn up at the palace, inquiring as to the girl's whereabouts. Children frequently choose this 'area of question' for further exploration. (I think there is a sense in which they feel the story has become rather risqué as a result of my emphasis on the girl being out all night.)

Think back to my Sam. This is the 'what's in it for them'. The 'what's in it for me' is a constructed opportunity for a wide range of language style and usage — not as an abstract exercise, but placed in a motivating context through the fiction we agree to create together. Now what about the territory in between? Discussion is needed here. There are things we have to think about: the idea of villagers turning up at the palace, what kind of reception they might get, what the palace protocol might be for receiving villagers, the room into which they might be shown to wait for the answer to their enquiries. I offer them one more idea to help shape their considerations: the premise that the way in which human beings elect to decorate the space they occupy can reveal something about the decisions they have made in that act of decoration, the values which affect their decision-making. In other words, that the presentation of a room is a projection of character.

The drama technique used here is usually called 'frozen picture' or 'still image'. Again, it reaches levels of greater sophistication than I have room to describe here — with further variations of subtlety it can be called 'tableau' or 'depiction', but basically, in this example small groups set about the task of using their own bodies to physically create the statues, paintings that the king might display in this ante-room in which the villagers had been asked to wait. On one occasion, a class started thinking faster than I did.'Wait a minute, though,' they said. 'A man like the king would probably be aware that what you put on the walls shows what kind of character you have. He'd probably know what we know. (That is, the real-life we.) We know from the rest of the story that he can be pretty cunning. If this is the room where he makes visitors wait he might have it decorated in such a way to give an impression of his character that might not necessarily be the true one!' A massive redrafting now took place. 'Portraits' of the king victorious in battle, stocking up the spoils of war were replaced by representations of acts of great kindness and generosity to humble villagers. What pleased me most was to see these children carefully applying the knowledge they had amassed from the story to a new situation: they gained an insight which had become transferable, a tool of previous experience being used to overcome new problems. Through looking at each other's efforts, and appropriate questioning and discussion, they built up an in depth picture for themselves not only as to what motivated the king, but also of the political, historical and social contexts in which Rumpelstiltskin might be understood.

You will have noted that what I have described so far is basically half of 'what is in it for me'. I want to break off for a moment to catalogue some of the developments in art work that can (and indeed have) arisen through this strategy. This building of context raises questions about the function of art. It has become the basis of visits to museums and galleries — not visits in the abstract, unconnected sense (it must do them good) but as a vital dynamic resourcing of their own creative work. It has prompted studies into portraiture, the work developing a further angle of perception through the insights that media educationists have given us — that choices have been made in the construction of representations that we see, and further, that those choices will have been made by people who do not always declare their interest, that those interests may have to be unravelled by us, the percipients. This seems to me to be immensely fertile ground for establishing a residency by a professional artist. I've not been fortunate enough to experience that kind of liaison myself but there are many first-rate accounts of how this might be achieved.[2] Many art teachers have made frequent use of the frozen picture strategy to prompt the children's own creative work in a broad variety of art media, and as a means of studying concepts like line, shape, composition. Display of the work arising from cross-curricular patterns of study such as this can become a teaching aid in its own right; a motivation, a sharing of ideas and a statement of the cultural ethos of the whole school. On one occasion, the children's own work, based on this one incident from the original story, turned the whole classroom into a replica of the King's ante-room.

Returning to our original drama of the villagers waiting in an ante-room to enquire about the girl's whereabouts now constituted a far richer experience for all of us concerned. It was not simply that now we had a good 'set' — although a set was certainly what it was. But what a set! The drama now took place as a highly sophisticated form of the double-think I was advocating earlier. The children's artwork which adorned the walls was not only highly skilled in its production, it was the result of deeply considered investigation of the motivations of the original story. It had been resourced by contact with the work of established artists, and analysed in respect of that most crucial consideration of media education: in whose *interest* is this meaning presented? These children had learned so much — yet now, in role again as the villagers, they gazed around the room in wonder, as if seeing all these things for the first time, and knowing nothing.

The temptation was there, of course, to simply put myself in role as the King, and challenge the 'villagers' head on. I think this would have been a useful approach, but I chose not to adopt it on this occasion. Instead, I joined the class in role as a fellow villager. A particular kind of villager, however. One who was overawed by the situation, who professed himself unable to understand the works of art around the room, who was worried that he wouldn't know how to behave when the King spoke to him, not to mention what he would say to the King. Now remember that the children actually understood *very well indeed* what was going on; they now used their knowledge selectively, projecting themselves into the personae of the villagers and sifting information until they came up with a version that they felt would be a villager's interpretation. A sustained effort at empathy; genuinely trying to see events through another person's eyes.

We were still waiting. We could use this time to prepare what we would say to the King; they could teach me how to behave if the King spoke to me. As a villager, I can tell them how I think I should speak to the King and make a real hash of it, in order to prompt them to correct me. The adoption of the villager's role makes it safer for me to teach by negative example. All right, I said, suppose I'm the King, what happens when I come in? This prompted a massive rehearsal of gesture and movement, tested for its appropriateness, and more significantly, an extended playing with the subtleties of language: should we say we have a complaint? or would it be better to make an enquiry? This is far more than vocabulary extension. These children were learning what it means to be strategic with language. And let's not forget the complexity of the situation. These children were faced with a visiting teacher, a relative stranger, pretending to be their teacher, pretending to be a villager, pretending to be the King. I maintain that handling all that when you are eight or nine years old is mind-expanding.

Our role as villagers gives us a further advantage: we can be critics of each other's efforts with an added umbrella of security. If someone makes a mess of their rehearsed speech to the King, it can be the villager we criticise, rather than the real person. These are humble villagers who could not really be expected to know courtly manners — indeed, I have already led the way myself. Within this framework, I shall have given opportunities for the kinds of language usage required by the Speaking and Listening Attainment Targets at Key Stages 1 & 2. For example: '...children need to work in a range of situations, with different stories and activities, developing their ability to ask questions, explain and present ideas, give and understand instructions, plan and discuss, tell stories and join in exploratory and collaborative play'.[3]

I offer here a micro-dot's worth of an immense power I have witnessed — an agenda for unleashing it more fully would need to consider:

- supporting teachers wishing to acquire and develop a broad range of teaching and learning styles. Essentially, these approaches thrive on negotiation between teacher and learners, the recognition of 'what's in it for them','what's in it for me', and the territory in-between;
- encouraging access to cross-curricular topics through that special kind of 'double think' promoted by entering the fiction and engaging with the art form;
- supporting the development of media education in all aspects of the curriculum, and ensuring that communication tasks are set within the contexts of a clearly defined audience and a re-cognised purpose;
- ensuring that children have the opportunity of first-hand ex-perience in a broad range of art media, both as participants and percipients;
- implementing the National Curriculum coherently, so that

Attainment Targets may be met through the vitality of cross-curricular patterns of study;
-   seeking to promote the cultural ethos of the school, through its display, presentation, cultural resourcing and sharing, both internally and through productive relationships with professional artists, museums and galleries and the local community.

These are tall orders. Fortunately, we do not have to wait for a golden age when they are commonplace in Primary education before we feel the benefit — the smallest-scale fumbling along this pathway can yield rich rewards and encourage more ambitious forays. Step out.

References

1   National Curriculum Council *Non-Statutory Guidance for English*, section 3:9.
2   See, for instance, the accounts in the *Arts in Schools Project* Newsletters.
3   National Curriculum Council *Non-Statutory Guidance for English*, section 2:0.

10 Developing science and technology programmes

Chris Jones

The introduction of Educational Support Grants by the Department of Education and Science led to a tremendous growth in the number of advisory teachers employed by LEAs.
Chris Jones spent three years as an ESG-funded advisory teacher helping to bring about change in primary school classrooms in the teaching of science and technology. Working in other people's classrooms is not easy, and Chris describes some of the organisational mechanisms and personal strategies needed to be employed to ensure that long-term and worthwhile gains were achieved.

Despite the sheer volume of print produced on primary science since the 1960s, and much more recently, primary technology, the evidence of HMI and other reports clearly indicate that although there were encouraging signs of progress in many parts of the country, it was still a case that too few children in primary schools were systematically introduced to science and technology. Twenty-five years of condemnation and advice from the printed page and the work of the 'Nuffield Junior Science Project' and the 'Schools' Council 5–13 Project' had not brought about significant advances. Only a minority of primary schools had effective programmes for the teaching and learning of science and technology.

There has been much speculation as to the reasons why, in

most primary schools, science has failed to take root and flourish. Suggestions have included: poor pre-service and in-service training; an image of science being 'lab coats, test tubes and mad professors'; far too sophisticated for the primary years; poor resources; uncertainty about science as a process/product; concerns, even fears, about classroom organisation and management; lack of general co-ordination within the school; and general inertia forces resisting change in the primary curriculum. Whatever factor or combination of factors conspired to prevent the development of science in the primary classroom there was a much stronger factor made up of external agencies that was determined to bring about change. A powerful means of executing change was provided to LEAs through the introduction of Educational Support Grants. Many LEAs submitted imaginative bids to the DES for the development of science, or science and technology, in their primary schools.

I was fortunate to be seconded to join a project funded through ESG money; I was to serve as a member of the team for three years. In planning their own overall support for primary science and technology, my own LEA developed a fully integrated approach, linking the ESG-funded activities within an already existing Curriculum Support Team. The general aim of my own authority's ESG project was to raise the level of teachers' knowledge, awareness, confidence and competence in the teaching and learning of primary science and technology. As part of that strategy, it was necessary to attempt to remove the 'mystique' from the subject and, more importantly, develop an approach to science and technology that was practical, investigative and problem-based providing fun for both teacher and child. Above all, the project team was charged with ensuring that science and technology became a permanent and integral part of the broad and balanced primary curriculum.

The project team consisted of three experienced 'support', rather than 'advisory', teachers. Our role was to support and nurture any level of science and technology that existed in the schools. Specifically we were: 'catalysts', 'facilitators', 'encouragers', 'enthusiasts', 'builders', 'exemplars of good practice', and 'change agents'. Team members were selected on the basis of the following criteria: above average classroom practitioners; had the ability to influence colleagues; had knowledge and experience of teaching in more than one school; had a 'good' INSET attendance record; had worked with adults and appreciated the fact that working in this way required different skills to 'normal' teaching; were adaptable; demonstrated initiative, creativity and imagination; and had sufficient expertise and experience to earn respect, and be respected, in the role of support teacher.

Schools, from time to time, may require help from such 'change agents', bringing the theory behind the practice and analyse with staff ways in which the change, or development, might be implemented, supporting its introduction, implementation and evaluation.

Sullivan[1] has shown that supporting change is not an easy business and it is vital that change agents have knowledge and experience of curriculum development and a wide knowledge of the learning environment. As important is the need for highly developed interpersonal skills and an awareness of others' sensibilities. The role of change agent is delicate and complicated, requiring a great deal of common sense and professionalism. The success of any innovation relies as much on relationships as on the quality of the ideas.

My three years were to be spent mainly in schools supporting science and technology initiatives for which schools had requested help. Being appointed carried with it mixed emotions. Had I put my credibility as a teacher and curriculum leader to the test? How were primary schools going to react to a classteacher who had only taught junior and secondary pupils but had no experience of teaching infants? How was I going to adjust to being one of the new 'missionaries'? What role was I to be expected to follow? What role would I be able to play? What role did I want to play? How was I going to cope with eating, drinking and sleeping primary science and technology for the next three years? What were the schools' expectations? What were the expectations of the inspectorate and DES? Schools that had requested support would be looking for sleeves rolled up, tie tucked in, practical help in introducing and/or implementing ideas in the classroom. Did I have the necessary qualities?

I was confident about what I considered to be good primary practice and how to match my support to the needs of colleagues and schools. I was also in a very fortunate position. My own authority had already established precedents and strategies for school-based support. No new structure had to be created, unlike other authorities. Such a framework was to be very useful to a novice. Previous support in my own authority had focused on the curriculum and staff and although I was to work with children, the aim was to improve the quantity and quality of science and technology teaching and learning. This meant I was concerned with trying to change colleagues' attitudes towards science and technology. It also entailed developing teachers' confidence, understanding and competence and with it their classroom practice. It was essential that I adopted a teacher-centred learning approach, rather than a child-centred approach, and I took on this role very easily.

With three years, initially, in which to do all this, I felt that I was going in at the deep end in September, 1985, but I knew that the water had been warmed as a result of previous school-based involvements and LEA support. I was confident in the framework in which I was to operate, I knew that I was well supported, I felt that I had the necessary qualities (otherwise I would not have been appointed). I knew something of the nature of 'curriculum and staff development', the role of change agents and the task that lay ahead.

Most schools have guidelines for most curriculum areas, including science, and to a lesser extent technology. I have supported schools in implementing such guidelines, but guarding against supporting and encouraging practices that I felt were misguided and inappropriate. This was a dilemma faced as a support teacher rather than the advisory teacher. Depending on the circumstances, including the personality of the classteacher, different strategies of persuasion were used to take a different course of action to the one that some classteacher had initially intended to follow. At times, I was viewed by a number of colleagues as perhaps bordering on the subversive — a claim that I would strongly deny. I have also supported schools in the review of schemes of work. In each case, the school had to be primed and ready for the support. Curriculum and staff development involves changing attitudes and practices of individual teachers within the whole organisation of the school. The process of change will only be effective if the school is fully committed and the staff willing to participate in what is considered to be a legitimate exercise and if the change agent appears to be fully informed of current practice and effectively involved with colleagues in schools. Any development is bound for failure unless staff believe in it and 'it is of them'. Curriculum development must not be handed to colleagues as products. Strategies must be sought which will closely involve all colleagues in the process of review and development, and allow and encourage them to move at their own pace and in response to their own needs and/or the needs of their pupils. The strategy must also seek to improve what is theirs by involving colleagues in re-thinking what they do rather than in trying to sell them new practices. The implementation of change requires support in terms of personnel, training, time and resources. There was sometimes a mistaken expectation by colleagues, including class teachers, curriculum leaders and headteachers that the ESG support team members would play the expert and produce wonderful 'curriculum packages' out of a hat, or act as 'super-teacher', undermining the work of a staff member. My own task was that of supporting the school's own efforts with staff and curriculum review and development, helping with cross-fertilisation of ideas and assisting in the identification and provision of adequate resources. As a support teacher, I was not prepared to supply schools with 'bolt-on' packages, nor take on the role of 'Father Christmas', handing out presents of extra materials and resources. Current practices and beliefs had to be discussed in some detail, questions asked, the answers examined and consideration given to appropriate action. This was a time-consuming task which involved many, if not all, the staff of a school.

Members of the inspectorate discussed with primary head-teachers, and still continue to do so, the issue of priorities for their schools within a framework of LEA provision. The approach was straightforward — headteachers were asked to identify priorities and to bid for support, agreeing to enter into an ensuing dialogue to determine specific aims, objectives, methodology and duration, resulting in a joint agreement on a particular area of review and development. The ESG team's method of operation was varied and included teaching side-by-side with colleagues in class, teaching groups of children, withdrawing teachers to work on specific areas, and taking classes to facilitate flexibility to enable in-school INSET to take place. The support team member's method of operation was to 'do things with colleagues and estab-lishments, not to them'. The whole purpose of the support was to develop the climate of thought, learning and co-operation and, above all, engender feelings of confidence.

In order to foster curriculum and staff development at the chalk face, and meet various needs, three broad strategies of sup-port were offered: school-based, centre-based and other types of support.

A high proportion of my time was spent in schools, support-ing colleagues in the introduction and implementation of primary science and technology. A total of three-and-a-half days per week was spent in this way.

School-based support was offered at a number of different levels. Category 'A' schools received a termly commitment of the equivalent of one day per week, or in some cases half a day per week, from the support team. An input of at least one term, possi-bly two, at this level of support was anticipated. Schools which had been within Category 'A' but no longer had a weekly commit-ment were classified as Category 'B'. In this instance a formal programme of less intensive follow-up support was agreed upon between the staff and support team. During this period I was actively involved in many activities including the following: establishing frameworks for dissemination throughout lower or upper schools; supporting the production of teacher and pupil materials; continuing to support staff development by way of practical workshops and/or staff discussions; helping in the setting-up of groups of cluster meetings of schools. The Category 'B' support continued the gradual retreat and the hopeful emergence of the self-determination on the part of the school and its staff.

Some schools received support other than Category 'A' and 'B'. These schools requested support but were usually unable to receive a concentrated form of input for one reason or another: the support team itself was fully committed for that term; the school's internal management structure would not support an involvement; or the staff themselves had not grasped the philosophy of curriculum development. In these cases, schools may have received a visit, or a series of visits, from a team member to help with resources or a scheme of work. In other instances practical workshops, coupled with key issue group discussions, would have been provided. Other schools requested Category 'C' support in terms of help in clarifying their own thoughts on particular issues, such as assessment and record-keeping. Some schools actually received Category 'C' support prior to receiving an 'A' input — the 'C' support was the necessary pump priming. Sixty-five per cent of my working week was spent working in Category 'A' schools, whose selection depended on them meeting a number of criteria: staff commitment to curriculum and staff development; science and technology identified as a GRIST priority; internal management structure to support and enable development; staff have attended recent INSET programmes with regard to science and technology; the staff perceived a need for the development.

School-based involvements were flexible and school-specific, but certain procedures were followed, namely: invitations/requests from the school; discussions not only with the headteacher but with all staff; familiarisation with the staff and children to establish relationships; defining an area of work; agreement of joint strategies and plans (objectives, methods of working, anticipated time-scale); planning of work; implementing work in the classroom; planning resources; classroom organisation and management; recording work; evaluating work; and facilitating the further implementation of the work after the withdrawal of the change agent.

Decisions on the level of involvement were made by the inspectorate. When a school was offered Category 'A' support, an intense period of discussion and negotiation commenced. In conjunction with staff, I had to carefully assess the existing practice in the school, carry out the curriculum and staff search, identify curriculum and staff needs and determine the 'where next'. This was no easy task. How do you go about reviewing existing practice, determining how effective present policy and practice really is, summarising the main conclusions and recommendations for review, development and implementation? Which is the best way to present findings and recommendations to all the staff, in a non-threatening way, and taking account of people's fears? Staff were also asked to consider the issue of monitoring and evaluation of the involvement. This required tact and diplomacy at the highest level.

It was imperative that the purposes of the involvement were conveyed to all staff in an open way. Despite this, there was frequently a sense of unease on the classteacher's behalf as to why they had been singled out for 'support'. Was it because their teaching was regarded as inadequate or because they were the soft target on the staff? Also, the fact that I was in the school as an ESG support teacher, and not there with some 'hidden evaluation and monitoring brief' was difficult for some classteachers to accept. The aim of the input was to share ideas. Some colleagues thought that at any moment I would drop the facade, I would turn green and sprout fangs in search of blood, or turn supergrass for an inquisitive inspector or headteacher. The first reaction of some colleagues was to offer me a group of children that I could work with in another classroom, in the corridor, the hall, the playground, the greenhouse, in fact anywhere but the classroom where I could not overlook the classteacher working with children. It took a great deal of trust and acceptance from some classteachers for me to get in alongside them in their own classroom.

Particulary at the beginning of the period of support, when the classteacher often lacked the confidence to attempt investigative work with their pupils, I was often observed at work by the classteacher. This often helped in establishing credibility as a competent teacher of children. In most cases, strategies were employed in which the classteacher took an increasing responsibility for the science and technology as the period of support progressed.

When working alongside colleagues in the classroom, the experiences presented to the children were collaboratively planned. Usually, although not always, a single group of children was involved with a scientific and/or technological element of the topic while the remaining group(s) tackled other topic-related work. This strategy was designed to develop and extend the classteacher's own teaching strategies in a non-threatening way. The classteacher was also encouraged to focus on the science and technology and I tried to guard against the situation where I was occupied with the science and technology group while the classteacher's attention was directed to the rest of the class. Such a situation would not have helped the professional or curriculum development sought.

Who was actually in charge in the classroom — the classteacher or the support teacher — was a question that troubled me on more than one occasion. How would Mr Grey have reacted had I disciplined someone in his group for behaving in a dangerous fashion? Would he have perceived this as 'interference' with his own classroom organisation and management? Luckily there was never a test case, although there were times when I felt uneasy about teachers' classroom management and control.

In most cases I shared the input with a colleagues from either the ESG project team or from the Curriculum Support Team. Working in tandem meant that a great deal of flexibility could be built into the involvement. One team member could be covering a class and the second support teacher holding detailed planning or evaluation discussions with the classteacher, curriculum leader, group of teachers and/or headteacher. The debriefing and planning sessions were essential so that we could evaluate the success, or otherwise, of the teaching and learning experiences. Both the support teachers could cover classes to release staff to observe good practice, either in another part of the school, or another school. Due to the team approach, it was essential that the support teachers held a similar set of beliefs as to what constitutes good primary practice.

Many of the school-based involvements combined work in the classroom with an input of some kind designed to help schools to develop a common approach to science and technology, or some aspect of science and technology. During involvements staff, either individually or collectively, asked for help in many aspects of the science and technology curriculum: the nature of primary science and technology; the nature of the problem-solving approach; identification of the processes, skills, attitudes and concepts associated with science and technology; questions as starting points for problem-solving and investigations; the experiences which could be presented to children; how the experiences should be presented; classroom organisation and management; topic planning; lesson planning; links between science and technology and other areas of the curriculum; progression and continuity; health and safety; assessment and record-keeping; the collection and storage of resources; policy formulation and staff development programmes. Such support focused not only upon the class teacher but also the curriculum leader to help them promote whole school development, or it actually involved working directly with the whole of the school staff. Since primary teachers frequently express a lack of confidence in the physical sciences and technology, the majority of my work in schools tended to focus on such areas, to the detriment of the biological sciences and some of the purely scientific processes and skills.

Support of this kind took place within the school itself, between schools in the cluster and during centre-based in-service courses and practical workshop sessions. During my period of secondment, I contributed to many schools' 'Baker INSET Days', and twilight sessions, encouraging whole staffs to embark upon a common planning theme for one term. Curriculum meetings were also used as opportunities to look at the common planning of scientific and technological work in the progression and continuity of skills and concepts. Practical workshops with whole staffs proved useful in providing a common focus for discussion within the school.

There was a small number of schools where relationships between staff members were strained and in some cases there was open hostility. In such circumstances, the whole school approach was put on its head and as a support teacher, I had to tread very carefully. One interesting activity was to identify the opinion-maker(s). There was usually one, possibly two, members of staff who exerted a strong influence on the ethos and working practices of the school. The natural leaders were not always the headteacher, deputy headteacher or 'B' allowances. They could include the school secretary, ancillary staff or caretaker. The natural leaders were one of the keys to making an involvement a success or a failure. It was important to win the right friends and influence the right people! There were other occasions when everything was just right — trust, confidence, professionalism were such that the exchange of ideas and the development of appropriate teaching and learning strategies led to the acquisition of new skills, knowledge, awareness and understanding on behalf of (most of) the staff.

As part of my role, I was involved in the organisation, management and delivery of various centre-based INSET courses and practical workshops. The courses and workshops differed in terms of audience, content and timing. All were open to headteachers and curriculum leaders, as their crucial roles were widely acknowledged. Courses targeted on many aspects of science and technology: Designing and Making, Control Technology, Problem-Solving; Classroom Organisation and Management; Science and Technology in the Early Years; Science and Technology in the Junior School. Longer courses, designed specifically for the curriculum leader, tackled many management issues such as: the effective leader; identifying and meeting curriculum and staff needs; organising and delivering staff meetings and practical workshops; resources; progression and continuity; assessment and record-keeping and towards a policy. A condition for acceptance on some of the non-specialist courses was that more than one teacher must attend from each school. This requirement provided the participant with support and back-up from within the school. Attendance at courses often arose from school-based involvements, or led to Category 'A' or 'C' support. It was always more difficult to assess the effectiveness of centre-based courses on classroom practice, despite the end-of-course evaluation questionnaires and 'where next'. I was happy running centre-based courses and workshops and see them as something which must go hand in hand with school-based support, but I was always happier when it came to assessing school-based support rather than centre-based support.

In my spare time, I worked with cluster groups of schools in order to examine the problems associated with transition, developed appropriate resource material for teachers and pupils, linked with and supported colleagues in other support agencies, both within and without the LEA, supported colleagues at the local College of High Education, and helped organise the annual LEA Science and Technology Fair.

On reflection, it took much of the first year of the project for me to develop into an effective change agent. Furthermore, in my own LEA, help did not reach all schools by the end of the three years. It was recognised from the outset that it would have been impossible to involve all schools effectively during the project and a conscious decision was made by the inspectorate to concentrate support in a few schools. I personally think that this was a correct decision — a number of schools received concentrated support, from which support could be disseminated to other link schools.

Throughout my time as a support teacher, my work was coordinated within the work of the Curriculum Support Team by the inspector with responsibility for that team, in consultation with the Science and Technology Inspector and the Chief Inspector. The support offered to colleagues was also monitored, assessed and evaluated in a number of ways at different levels: biweekly steering group meetings; observation of the support teacher's work by members of the inspectorate; regular planning and evaluation meetings involving support teachers and colleagues in schools, and support teachers, staff and members of the inspectorate; feedback from pastoral inspectors; questionnaire returns; and external evaluation.

The actual involvement in each school was monitored,

assessed and evaluated using the specification of clear initial objectives to be achieved and the close monitoring of outcomes. At the commencement of each involvement a written contract was made between the school and the team.

It is difficult to base predictions about long-term changes, but in the short term an increased number of children were involved in practical, investigative and problem-based science and technology. Support in the classroom enabled children, and teachers, to undertake purposeful, practical activities within the framework of the children's own experience. Many colleagues saw this approach as a more effective way of communicating the nature of primary science and technology rather than the lecture or seminar conducted away from the classroom, in the absence of children.

In order to assess the effectiveness of the support offered to colleagues in greater detail, I attempted to identify those aspects which signified a real change in the teaching and learning of science and technology. I looked for an increase in certain activities, using an *aide-memoire* which classified the support into five main areas: the curriculum; implementation; facilities and resources; staff development and philosophy. The monitoring attempted to identify the effect the school-based support was having rather than recording what teachers were already doing. I did not comment where it was obvious that the teacher already used a practical and purposeful approach to science and technology. In order to monitor effectively, it was necessary to include individual classes and the school as a whole.

There were many positive signs that the school-based support strategy adopted had had a positive effect on a particular teacher and a school. Changes in attitude were reflected in colleagues' willingness to consider new ideas and a desire to 'change'. Many curriculum leaders were developing confidence in their ability to become co-ordinators and change agents themselves. In a large number of classrooms, there was an increased motivation on behalf of the teacher to improve the quality of their own performance in class and a keenness to promote science and technology throughout the school. Classrooms reflected moves towards child-centred learning, changes in teaching style and classroom organisation and the asking of open-ended questions. In other classes, the non-user-friendly 'physical' concepts were tackled with interest, including: 'structures'; 'energy'; 'control'; 'electricity' and 'magnetism', giving breadth and balance to the science and technology curriculum. In some staffrooms there was an increased interest in science and technology shown by requests from staff for appropriate courses, workshops, resources, and teacher and pupil materials. In a great number of schools, INSET took place during twilight sessions and curriculum meeting-time was devoted to produce effective record-keeping systems and formulate policies. In some establishments, the headteacher effectively supported the curriculum leader during curriculum development meetings, showed an active interest in the classroom, provided resources and actually released the curriculum leader for internal support work, enabling curriculum and staff development to continue throughout the week and term.

The pointers listed above were some indicators, although by no means all, that primary science and technology was going along the right lines. Many colleagues will see that these are inseparable from good primary practice and not solely characteristic of science and technology. I would agree and I take the view that good primary science and technology is, above all, good primary practice. I did not find all, or even most of the pointers on my *aide-memoire* in all schools. The presence, however, of a few in schools which, prior to the ESG input, had little experience of science and technology teaching and learning was very encouraging. Where no increase came about, and in at least one classroom this was so, continued support is paramount, especially from within the school itself.

Support of this kind did much to prepare the ground for the coming of the National Curriculum proposals and its associated issues.

I am not quite sure who gained most from my secondment; the schools that I was supposed to be assisting, myself or my present school. I enjoyed working in other people's schools; there was a cross-fertilisation of ideas. I developed new skills, enthusiasms and knowledge which I have found more than useful in my present role as deputy headteacher of a primary school.

In order to continue the development of science and technology programmes in primary schools, particulary in the light of the National Curriculum and SEAC proposals, there clearly needs to be some form of continuing support in the future. The support needs to be targeted at different audiences, using different strategies and concentrating on different issues in order to build on and extend previous support and initiatives, and to help schools introduce and implement the latest proposals.

The key target areas are the classteachers themselves, the curriculum leaders, the headteachers and the cluster/pyramid groups of schools.

Classteachers, and perhaps some curriculum leaders, need support through in-service training to extend their own knowledge and understanding of science and technology, but also opportunities to develop their primary classroom expertise. Practical courses must be provided which continue to introduce, explain and use many of the basic concepts in physics, earth science, chemistry, biology and technology, designed to make the course participants more knowledgeable about a wide range of modern scientific and technological theories and more familiar with some of the techniques of investigational and problematic science and technology. The Open University 'Science Foundation Course, S102' is tailor-made. LEAs need to provide resources to enable teachers to attend these courses. Similar, less intensive courses, need to be provided locally, either as centre-based courses or as school-based courses by the local authority support agencies.

There is a need for in-service support for curriculum leaders in primary schools to develop them as effective change agents. The emphasis which is being given increasingly to curriculum management in schools is reflected in the management role expected of curriculum leaders. This must continue to be reflected in the in-service courses offered to curriculum leaders in the future. Courses must include management components which actively engage the participants in the task of co-ordinating science and technology in their own schools. Tasks must be designed to enable the curriculum leader to monitor and assess science and technology throughout the school. Curriculum leaders must be encouraged, and allowed, to develop their managerial skills.

Headteachers themselves may need support in determining how to fully implement the latest proposals, or simply to be reassured that they are heading in the right direction.

A number of cluster/pyramid groups of schools will need support when they deal with the issues of assessment, record-keeping, moderation and reporting.

The scale of the task is great. In some schools considerable changes are needed in classroom practice to enable the introduction and implementation of the National Curriculum and SEAC proposals. Help will be needed, of a less intensive kind, not just to get science and technology going, but to tackle issues such as progression and continuity, and resources. Support must be made available. A National Curriculum Support Team has emerged within my own authority and I believe that such an agency of change has the ability to support colleagues in schools, enhance primary curriculum development and promote good primary practice.

The DES, NCC, SEAC, LEAs, inspectors/advisors, support agencies, governors, parents, headteachers, curriculum leaders and classteachers all have responsibilities which go beyond the provision of learning experiences and material resources. Schools should always be in a state of intellectual change and development. We all need to foster a climate within schools which values co-operation, not competition, and which promotes innovation. Everyone concerned with education has a responsibility to plan an educational system, but also to help individual schools and colleagues to grow and develop. We must create new opportunities and improve provision and tap enthusiasm and expertise. We must create a climate which allows schools and individuals to develop and to promote a framework within which it can happen. It requires an openness on the part of everyone concerned about what the national and local priorities are and what the views of its establishments are. Policies have to be communicated to schools in ways which will ensure that they are accepted, understood and internalized.

We are faced with a mammoth and urgent INSET task to reach large numbers of teachers rapidly. LEAs may well focus their in-service provision onto centre-based courses. Legislation demands that science and technology be taught. Unless there is some practical support within the classroom to help teachers come to terms with the new demands then these changes may well be a distortion of intentions. Even short-term classroom-based support is an expensive resource, but whether provided through an external agency or through timetabling support from the school's curriculum leader, it is a resource that a successful school cannot be without.

Reference

1 Sullivan, M. (1987) 'Working and Learning in Other People's Classrooms' *Education 3–13*, 15(7).

11 Supporting change and development — key themes

Ann Lewis

'A leader is a dealer in hope'
Napoleon

There runs, through each chapter in this book, a shining thread. This is an insistence on grasping opportunities for change and responding imaginatively. These accounts describe teachers and heads being proactive, shaping children's educational experiences in line with what those professionals regard as 'good practice'. The 1988 Education Reform Act has provided a cloak of consensus but beneath that cloak there is room for individuality.

Key themes

A number of common themes emerge from these accounts. These themes point to some of the characteristics that underlie successful change and development in our schools. The themes can be summarised as leadership, collective responsibility, flexibility and imagination.

Leadership

All the writers refer, implicitly or explicitly, to the characteristics of effective leadership. One characteristic of effective leadership is the fostering of others' confidence. The head of a school must foster the professional confidence of all those working in the school. Similarly, curriculum co-ordinators, advisory teachers and support teachers need to have a quality of supporting other teachers without, as Chris Jones notes, making the co-teacher feel that he or she has been picked out to receive support because of inadequacies in his or her teaching. It is striking how frequently the writers here comment on the need for sensitivity when working with colleagues. Teachers can also, as Mike Sullivan and Ruth Merttens observe, be crucial in fostering parents' confidence in developing children's learning at home.

To develop confidence in others requires a degree of professional *self*-confidence. Several of the writers here describe 'putting themselves on the line' as a nerve-racking but necessary part of leadership and the promotion of change. For heads, support and advisory teachers this may involve being seen to be teaching, not just advising. This is particularly so if the teaching approaches being advocated are in some way 'risky'. David Sheppard's approach to integrated arts work using a 'frozen picture' technique must surely have been received more sympathetically when teachers could see, not just hear about, the approach. Teachers who have professional self-confidence will be prepared to reveal details about themselves as people with lives outside the classroom. This smooths relationships with both children and their parents. Confident teachers are not afraid of letting go of control of the learning process: to other teachers, to parents or, as in the Arts in Schools Projects, to the children themselves.

Confidence is linked with clarity about educational goals. Research into the characteristics of effective schools (e.g. Rutter et al., 1979;[1] Mortimore et al., 1988[2]) has highlighted the importance of leadership associated with clear goals. The same point is made in these chapters. For example, Brenda Lofthouse (pp.44/49) notes,

> 'The head should have vision of the total curriculum in terms of content, delivery and ethos... All curriculum developments have to be planned like a campaign of attack. The advantage should always be with the head because she/he knows it is coming'.

This clarity of vision is evident in the accounts of successful change in the context of the development of whole school policies, work with parents, collaborative work with other teachers, and trying out new learning methods with children. Pursuit of these goals requires persistence and, perhaps, some subversiveness. Clear vision enables the facilitator to recognise that small steps towards the goal are not a cop-out but realistic progress towards the target.

Another aspect of effective leadership for change is a concern with the development of teachers' career paths. Bringing about change in a school may require a 'paradigm shift'. This will have repercussions for teachers' practice. For example, a new commitment to collaborative teaching will have an impact on where and how the teacher wishes to work in future. The way in which change is bought about may encourage teachers to work in a certain way. For example, to pursue action research strategies or to use professionals, both within and outside the school, as consultants. Responding to change has now become an integral part of school life and so teachers have been presented, by senior staff, with various ways of dealing with this. So the process of change is important, not just in itself, but also as a model for the next generation of change agents. In addition, the process of becoming an agent of change affects careers. This may in itself prompt teachers towards a particular role, for example, away from full-time class teaching and towards inspectorial work or headship.

Collective responsibility

An emphasis on collective responsibility may seem at odds with the stress on clear leadership. However, all the writers emphasise that effective change requires the change agent to work with others and to coax, rather than to bludgeon, them on to his or her side. At school level, collective responsibility is linked with ownership of the change. Teachers will go along with change more readily if it is seen to be at least partly the result of their own choices. David Winkley suggests using a diverse range of 'consultants' from within and outside the school to foster this sense of the whole school setting the agenda and making the decisions.

Developing collective responsibility for the curriculum can, as many of these accounts show, be a very effective way of breaking down barriers and isolation within and between schools. However, collective responsibility may be an empty claim, masking an absence of real commitment to change. If something is everyone's responsibility it may slide into being nobody's.

Developing collective responsibility is, as Sally Davies acknowledges, often easier in smaller schools. However Jim Campbell and Brenda Lofthouse discuss possible impediments to establishing genuine collaboration in curriculum planning. These may be linked with the extensive demands placed on curriculum coordinators or the nature of individuals who revel in blocking any change.

Collaboration has become, as Moyra Bentley discussed, a

platitude in primary education — a self-evident good which is rarely challenged. There are reservations about 'collaboration'. It may be very time-consuming and be rejected on those grounds by some staff. This reservation should be taken seriously. Is the time spent collaborating with others necessarily justified by end results? Honesty is required when considering such questions. Change may be carried out for a number of reasons (including self-glorification and approval by inspectors) but ultimately the only valid justification is a considered belief that the change will improve children's education.

Collective responsibility for the curriculum can also be considered in relation to parents and teachers. This is another area where rhetoric often outruns reality. 'Parental involvement' is surely a self-evident good, who could be against it? In practice parents are often treated as a long way behind the school in terms of their role in fostering learning. This is another occasion for teachers to confront some hard questions. Do we really want parents in the classroom and teaching children? What kinds of things can parents be 'safely' given to do with their children at home? Mike Sullivan has discussed both questions and possible answers in this area. The low expectations of parents by teachers found in Barbara Tizard's research (Tizard et al.,1988[3]) are countered by accounts here of the IMPACT project. It has been said that the National Curriculum is demonstrating that teachers have tended to have expectations of children which are too low. Similarly, the IMPACT project indicates that teachers may be under-estimating the kinds of activities which the large majority of parents can and will do with their children to develop and reinforce school-based learning.

Another aspect of collective responsibility is a responsibility for learning which is shared between teachers and children. This is implicit in several of the earlier chapters in this book and is brought out strongly in David Sheppard's account of integrated arts work in primary schools. There has been much debate about whether or not 'child-centred' approaches are possible within the National Curriculum. This debate has taken place at both theoretical and practical levels (see, for example, Kelly 1990[4] and Wilson 1991,[5] respectively). Accounts such as those by David Sheppard provide ideas about how we might sustain child-initiated work within the framework of the National Curriculum.

Mike Sullivan uses the phrase 'Everyone taking part and everyone winning a prize'(p.114) in relation to parents' involvement in their children's education. It can be applied also in the much wider context of how schools in these accounts are changing. 'Everyone taking part' means all teachers, all parents, all children, and a diverse range of consultants picked for what they have to offer the school.

Flexibility

The recent educational climate has been one in which schools have been forced to make changes, not only in curricula but in relation to finance, governors and relations with parents. The distinction between 'given' (i.e. unchangeable) and 'policy' variables (i.e. open to change) (Davies, p.34) is helpful. People who can retain flexibility without losing sight of their educational goals and principles should be highly valued in this climate. HMI's surveys of the implementation of the National Curriculum (e.g. HMI 1989,[6] 1990[7]) show that schools have not ignored pressures to change but have, in general, addressed these directly.

One illustration of the kinds of change taking place is the 'galloping inflation' (Campbell, p.10) in the range and complexity of roles taken by curriculum co-ordinators in primary schools. Similar change has taken place in the roles of advisory and support teachers. Change is intrinsic to life and an educational system which is alive must continue to develop. Not to change in response to the changing climate is to ensure the death of the organism. So we should see change as healthy and enabling not as a threat.

Imagination

To accept the inevitability of change, to plan for change while keeping faith with strongly held educational principles and then to implement change is at the heart of the earlier chapters in this book. All the contributors write from experiences of bringing about change in schools. The accounts are rooted in what has been tried, perhaps found to be problematic, re-tried and ultimately found to be workable and worthwhile. The work in rural schools, described by Moyra Bentley, epitomises a response to change characterised by imaginative resolution of the challenges. The workers in that project have found effective ways of, for example, sharing resources and developing curricula.

The education system in this country has been characterised by teachers' initiatives. Many exciting and innovative ideas have sprung from teachers and heads reflecting on practice, not being merely passive recipients of accepted wisdom or local edicts. Michael Armstrong's (1980)[8] and Stephen Rowlands' (1984)[9] writings illustrate this approach. It is a feature of our system which has attracted bemused awe from visitors from highly centralised and externally regulated education systems. The development of action research in classrooms, espoused by John Elliott and others (Elliott and Ebbutt, 1985;[10] Hopkins, 1985[11]) is another illustration of this tradition. Eric Dodd suggests ways of linking such work with teacher appraisal. Here again is an example of imaginative response to change.

Conclusion

Change is happening fast, but this does not make it a new phenomenon. Thirty years ago Dean Rusk wrote that 'The pace of events is moving so fast that unless we can find some way to keep our sights on tomorrow, we cannot expect to be in touch with today'. There are imaginative responses to fostering development in schools which have an eye on tomorrow. Supporting change and development in schools requires leadership, courage and vision from all engaged in primary education.

References

1   Rutter, M., Maughan, B., Mortimore, P. and Ouston, J. (1979) *Fifteen Thousand Hours* Open Books, London.
2   Mortimore, P., Sammons, P. Stoll, L., Lewis, D. and Ecob, R.(1988) *School Matters* Open Books, Wells.
3   Tizard, B., Blatchford, P., Burke, J., Farquar, C. and Plewis, I. (1988) *Young Children at School in the Inner City* Lawrence Erlbaum Associates, London.
4   Kelly V. (1990) *The National Curriculum: A Critical Review* Paul Chapman, London.
5   Wilson, J. (1991)'Children, Choice and the National Curriculum', *Education 3–13* 19(1) pp. 18–22
6   HMI (1989) *The implementation of the National Curriculum in Primary Schools* DES, London.
7   HMI (1990) *The implementation of the National Curriculum in Primary Schools: A survey of 100 Schools* DES, London.
8   Armstrong, M. (1980) *Closely Observed Children* Writers and Readers, London.
9   Rowlands, S. (1984) *The Enquiring Classroom* Falmer, Lewes.
10 Elliott, J. and Ebbutt D. (1985) *Facilitating Educational Action Research in Schools* Longman, London.
11 Hopkins, D. (1985) *A Teacher's Guide to Classroom Research* Open University, Milton Keynes.

Index